The Seal of Orestes

Greek Studies: Interdisciplinary Approaches
General Editor: Gregory Nagy, Harvard University

The Seal of Orestes

Self-Reference and Authority in Sophocles' *Electra*

ANN G. BATCHELDER

ROWMAN & LITTLEFIELD PUBLISHERS, INC.

ROWMAN & LITTLEFIELD PUBLISHERS, INC.

Published in the United States of America
by Rowman & Littlefield Publishers, Inc.
4720 Boston Way, Lanham, Maryland 20706

3 Henrietta Street
London WC2E 8LU, England

British Cataloging in Publication Information Available

Library of Congress Cataloging-in-Publication Data

Batchelder, Ann G.
The seal of Orestes :   self-refernce and authority in Sophocles'
Electra / Ann G. Batchelder.
p.   cm.
Includes bibliographical references and index.
1. Sophocles. Electra. 2. Sophocles--Knowledge--Performing arts.
3. Electra (Greek mythology) in literature. 4. Orestes (Greek
mythology) in literature. 5. Art and literature--Greece--History.
6. Performing arts in literature. 7. Authority in literature.
8. Theater in literature. I. Title.
PA4413.E5B38 1994 882'.01--dc20 94-40447 CIP

ISBN 0–8476–7990–X (cloth : alk. paper)
ISBN 0–8476–7991–8 (pbk. : alk. paper)

Printed in the United States of America

⊖™ The paper used in this publication meets the minimum requirements of
American National Standard for Information Sciences—Permanence of
Paper for Printed Library Materials, ANSI Z39.48–1964.

Contents

Greek Studies: Interdisciplinary Approaches

Foreword

by Gregory Nagy, General Editor

Building on the foundations of scholarship within the disciplines of philology, philosophy, history, and archaeology, this series spans the continuum of Greek traditions extending from the second millennium B.C. to the present, not just the archaic and classical periods. The aim is to enhance perspectives by applying various different disciplines to problems that have in the past been treated as the exclusive concern of a single given discipline. Besides the crossing-over of the older disciplines, as in the case of historical and literary studies, the series encourages the application of such newer ones as linguistics, sociology, anthropology, and comparative literature. It also encourages encounters with current trends in methodology, especially in the realm of literary theory.

Of all the extant dramas of Sophocles, the *Electra* stands out as perhaps the most problematic for the modern reader to appreciate as literature. *The Seal of Orestes: Self-Reference and*

Authority in Sophocles' Electra, by Ann G. Batchelder, reaches a new level in our literary appreciation of this drama by treating it as exactly that, drama, not just literature. We ordinarily think of self-reference as a literary device, where literature refers to literature. But in this play the "self" of the self-reference is not just literature, that is, the poetry of Sophocles: it is theater itself, the medium that makes the poet's composition come to life in performance. More than that, the theater that serves as historical context for the self-references of Sophocles' *Electra* is none other than the State Theater of Athens.

In archaic Greek poetics, the concept of an author depends on the author's authority, which is signaled by such visible signs as a signet ring or seal, that is, a **sphragis**. A notable example is line 19 of Theognis, where that poet speaks of his **sphragis** of authority. With his seal, the figure of Theognis authorizes himself, making himself the author. To be an author of drama in State Theater, however, goes beyond purely literary authorship: in this case, the authority of the State itself authorizes the author. This concept is dramatized by Sophocles' *Electra* in the form of the **sphragis** or seal of Orestes, which becomes a visible sign of this hero's emerging authority as the legitimate Head of State. As Batchelder's book demonstrates, the hero's **sphragis** authorizes him to take control—of not only the State but also his own drama. In this way, the Seal of Orestes actually symbolizes the drama.

As Batchelder's book goes on to show, the Seal of Orestes conveys two levels of successful authorization and authorship: inside the dramatic frame, Orestes takes control of the state—and of his own drama—as he competes with his rivals for control, while Sophocles himself maintains ultimate control of the frame from the outside, as the definitive dramaturge. In its self-references, Sophocles' *Electra* refers simultaneously to stagecraft and statecraft—not just poetic craft.

In the classical era of Athens, the premier form of State Theater was tragedy. Tragedy was also the premier medium of poetic craft. In the language of tragedy's stepsister, comedy, it was enough to say "the craft"—that is, **tekhnê**—to refer to tragedy. As we see from the ubiquitous references to *the* **tekhnê** in the *Frogs* of Aristophanes, the medium of tragedy is in fact "the craft" par excellence. The Seal of Orestes in the tragedy of the *Electra* becomes the signature of this craft.

Theater combines sight with sound, visualization with verbalization. State Theater is thus inherently spectacular, a visual realization of the State's dazzling authority. The very idea of spectacle is inherent in the word for theater, **theatron**, derived from **theaomai** 'see, be a spectator'. As the centerpiece of State Theater, tragedy is the most spectacular of all media of performance in classical Athens. By virtue of its status as the ultimate theater, tragedy can present itself as the ultimate spectacle of the State.

Orestes becomes the successful author, producer, and director of his own ultimate spectacle, his own drama, culminating in the Messenger Speech of the *Electra*. The dramatic illusion that he authorizes has the effect of transforming the poetics of epic into the poetics of theater, much as Athenian State Theater historically transformed the sum total of epic traditions into its own authorized repertoire. Pursuing this fundamental insight, Batchelder's book traces the many ways in which Sophocles has fashioned the Seal of Orestes, the visible sign of the hero's political authority, into a unique symbol for the poetic authority of theater itself.

Acknowledgments

I wish to thank the many who have helped me in completing this book. I am grateful for the technical assistance given in the early stages by Robert and Holly Doyle, Michael Weishan, and friends at the Perseus Project, including Kenneth Morrell and Gregory Crane. Thanks also to Nancy Andrews for sharing her insights and love of literature and to Roger Ceragioli, teaching colleague and kind friend. Special and warmest thanks to Emily Vermeule for her support, interest, and inspiring presence. I am indebted also to my colleagues at the College of the Holy Cross for providing a stimulating and congenial environment in which to complete this project and to the College itself for the generous research leave granted in the fall of 1992. Many, many thanks to Paul Deane and Phyllis Horn Deane, gentlest and finest of critics. My debt to Gregory Nagy, and my great admiration for him, are evident in the pages that follow. I feel the deepest gratitude to all of my family, including M. S. and C. C. Batchelder, and most especially, to the truly nearest and dearest, who make all good things in my life possible, Sally A. Batchelder, Aaron E. Sunstein, and Bruce D. Sunstein.

The death of Aegisthus as represented on the Boston Oresteia Krater, a red-figure calyx krater attributed to the Dokimasia Painter. (Courtesy of the Museum of Fine Arts, Boston, 63.1246, William Francis Warden Fund)

Introduction

In the illustration of the death of Aegisthus found on the Boston Oresteia Krater, a red-figure calyx krater attributed to the Dokimasia Painter, Orestes strides forth, sword drawn, about to kill Aegisthus, who is shown seated on the throne. The death of Aegisthus is not an uncommon subject in vase painting, but there is an unusual element in this particular composition. At the moment before his death, Aegisthus is usually shown seated on a very ornate throne, with empty hands, "a symbol of usurped position and empty authority."[1] This painting, however, shows Aegisthus with one hand stretched forth in supplication, the other drawn back holding a lyre "parallel to the floor, as though not to damage it."[2] The artist portrays Aegisthus as the man who, prior to Orestes' entrance, has been seated on the throne, playing the lyre. At the moment of death—he is shown already wounded—he is supplicating for his life with one hand and drawing back the lyre, almost protectively, with the other.

---

[1] Vermeule 1966.5, the article in which she describes and discusses the significance of the vase (Boston, Museum of Fine Arts, 63.1246). See also Davies 1969, which includes bibliography of other discussions of the vase.
[2] Vermeule 1966.5.

1

The image of Aegisthus as the lyre player is a minor but persistent theme in vase painting.[3] The portrayal of Aegisthus as both musician and king, present in the visual arts, is one more fully developed in drama in Sophocles' play the *Electra*. I propose that in this play Sophocles presents Aegisthus and Orestes as two rival dramatists, each competing to gain, or maintain, political control through poetic art. Each uses the power of words and the illusions of the theater to establish his authority in the community.

In the recognition scene of Sophocles' *Electra* we see how Sophocles' version of the Orestes myth differs from that of his predecessors. In Aeschylus' version Orestes reveals his identity to Electra by locks of hair, footprints, and fabric woven by Electra herself. These tokens are signs of the connection between Orestes and Electra. Of other, now lost, versions that preceded Sophocles' (including those of Hesiod, Xanthus, Stesichorus, and Simonides), we know something of the recognition scene only in the case of Stesichorus. A papyrus fragment of a commentary on his poem indicates that here too the lock of hair was used in the recognition scene (Stesichorus PMG 217). In Euripides' *Electra*, which may have preceded Sophocles' version, it is interesting to note that it is the scar on Orestes' brow, a reminder of a childhood accident, that identifies him. While chasing a fawn in the courtyard with Electra, he slipped, and the scar of the resulting cut remains. In all these versions the token of identification is one that connects Orestes and Electra through shared physical resemblance or shared childhood experience.

But in Sophocles' *Electra* the token is of a different kind. It marks the connection, not between Orestes and Electra, but between Orestes and Agamemnon. It is the **sphragis** 'signet ring' of his father that identifies Orestes. The signet ring

---

[3]   Vermeule 1966.5 and 1987.130

authenticates his connection with Agamemnon, the rightful ruler of Mycenae, and thus connects Orestes with the traditional and rightful source of authority in the community.

I suggest that Sophocles uses the recognition scene to show what distinguishes his version of the Orestes myth from those of others, to say what establishes this version of the story as his own. His interest, unlike that of Aeschylus and Euripides, is not in the question of matricide, but in the nature of the artist and the authority of the poetic voice in the community. Sophocles' Orestes is an Odyssean figure, the king who returns in disguise to test the community through use of the **ainos** 'an allusive tale, containing an ulterior purpose'[4] and to punish the usurpers of the king. Just as Odysseus used stories and the disguise of a beggar to reestablish his authority in Ithaca, so Sophocles' Orestes uses the art of poetry and the illusions of the theater to restore the true voice of authority in Mycenae. When Orestes reveals his identity to Electra, he indicates, with the signet ring of his father, that he is the inheritor not only of the kingship, but also of the poetic tradition. The recognition scene reveals both the identity of Orestes and the nature of the play the *Electra*. It is a play about playwrights and the art of writing the play.

The first chapter, "The Rehearsal," discusses the opening scene of the play as a rehearsal for the drama that the Paidagogos and Orestes will stage to deceive Clytemnestra and Aegisthus. It examines the relationship of the Paidagogos to Orestes in terms of the older artist guiding the younger poet, just as the dramatist Sophocles was guided by the poetic tradition of Homer.

The second chapter, "Different Voices, Different Stories," considers Clytemnestra and Electra as rival poets of praise and blame, each trying to establish as true her own version of the

---

[4] For this definition of the **ainos** see Verdenius 1962.389. See also Pucci 1977.76 and Nagy 1979.235-42.

past, the story of Agamemnon's death. We see the two women locked in a contest of words, a contest that will not be resolved until Aegisthus and Orestes enter into their own poetic competition.

The third chapter, "The Play Begins," is an examination of the false story of Orestes' death as told to Clytemnestra and Electra by the Paidagogos. Here we see Orestes' false tale, which is believed by all, assume an authority beyond that of either Clytemnestra's or Electra's version of the past. In creating the messenger speech of the Paidagogos, Orestes transforms the epic language of Homer into the dramatic poetry of the theater. He creates a drama in order to deceive and ultimately overcome Clytemnestra and Aegisthus. With the ringing, epic tones of the Paidagogos' speech, Orestes creates a fiction more powerful and compelling than truth.

The fourth and last chapter, "The Final Contest," concerns the final scenes of the play. It considers the significance of the **sphragis**, the seal on the signet ring of Orestes, as a recognition token for both Orestes and the play itself. The chapter concludes with a discussion of the last scene of the play as a dramatic contest between the two competing playwrights, Orestes and Aegisthus, the dramatic contest in which Orestes triumphantly establishes political and poetic authority in Mycenae.

CHAPTER 1

The Rehearsal

In the opening scene of Sophocles' *Electra*, we are introduced to the relationship between the Paidagogos and Orestes. The Paidagogos has been the teacher and protector of Orestes in exile, and the play opens as he, having guided Orestes home, identifies the landmarks of Mycenae. At first the Paidagogos appears to be in charge, but as the scene progresses, Orestes asserts himself and begins to take control. He describes his strategy for restoring the rightful kingship of Mycenae and instructs the Paidagogos in his role in the plan. The Paidagogos will play the part of the messenger from Phocis who will announce the death of Orestes. This speech, as we shall later see, is the most Homeric of the entire play. Orestes will use the artistry of the older man—his ability to describe a fatal chariot race so vividly that it will seem to be true—as part of a larger, artistic deception. In this first scene we see the development of the artist from the man who follows his teacher, the older poet, to the man who masters the older poet's art and makes it part of his own.

We can begin to see in this scene that Sophocles' *Electra* is a play about play-writing.[1] Orestes will use the poet's tradition and art to restore justice to the community, by playing the role of the traditional Athenian playwright. He will be, like the fifth-century tragedian, the writer, director, and actor in his own creation. Sophocles, in presenting Orestes as a playwright, creating his own play before our eyes, is giving us a picture of the fifth-century dramatist. As playwright, Orestes is part of the larger poetic tradition of the artist as authority figure who, through his art, restores justice, or **dikê** (δίκη). Orestes is a figure like Odysseus in epic, or like the self-representations of Hesiod, Solon, and Theognis in wisdom poetry—figures who use the power and authority of their craft to restore the traditional values of their communities.

Let us start with Odysseus. Orestes is like Odysseus, the king who returns in disguise to test the community through **ainoi** (e.g., *Odyssey* 14.191-359; 17.415-44) and to punish the usurpers of the king.[2] Disguised as a beggar, Odysseus tells the Cretan lies, false stories of himself and his wanderings, stories that he uses to hide his own identity until he is able to effect his revenge. He uses the art of the poet to tell these tales, as Eumaeus reveals when he describes the beggar to Penelope:

> ὡς δ' ὅτ' ἀοιδὸν ἀνὴρ ποτιδέρκεται, ὅς τε θεῶν ἔξ
> ἀείδη δεδαὼς ἔπε' ἱμερόεντα βροτοῖσι,

---

[1] For examples of discussions of self-reference in tragedy and bibliography, see Dodds 1966.46-47; Segal 1982.215-71 and 1986.97-106; Foley 1985.205-58, and Albert Henrichs in a forthcoming article " 'Why Should I Dance': Ritual Self-referentiality in the Choral Odes of Greek Tragedy," in which he discusses at length self-reference in Sophocles. See also Segal 1980/81.136-37 and 1981.287-90 on the urn in Sophocles' *Electra* as a metatragic symbol.

[2] For the **ainos** as 'an allusive tale, containing an ulterior purpose', see p. 3n4 above.

τοῦ δ᾽ ἄμοτον μεμάασιν ἀκουέμεν, ὁππότ᾽ ἀείδῃ·
ὡς ἐμὲ κεῖνος ἔθελγε παρήμενος ἐν μεγάροισι.

Odyssey 17.518-21

But as when a man looks to a singer, who has been given
from the gods the skill with which he sings for delight of mortals,
and they are impassioned and strain to hear it when he sings to them,
so he enchanted me in the halls as he sat beside me.[3]

At the very moment of regaining his authority, just as
Odysseus strings the bow, the images of poet and king
combine:[4]

αὐτίκ᾽ ἐπεὶ μέγα τόξον ἐβάστασε καὶ ἴδε πάντῃ,
ὡς ὅτ᾽ ἀνὴρ φόρμιγγος ἐπιστάμενος καὶ ἀοιδῆς
ῥηιδίως ἐτάνυσσε νέῳ περὶ κόλλοπι χορδήν,
ἅψας ἀμφοτέρωθεν ἐυστρεφὲς ἔντερον οἰός,
ὣς ἄρ᾽ ἄτερ σπουδῆς τάνυσεν μέγα τόξον Ὀδυσσεύς.
δεξιτερῇ δ᾽ ἄρα χειρὶ λαβὼν πειρήσατο νευρῆς·
ἡ δ᾽ ὑπὸ καλὸν ἄεισε, χελιδόνι εἰκέλη αὐδήν.
μνηστῆρσιν δ᾽ ἄρ᾽ ἄχος γένετο μέγα, πᾶσι δ᾽ ἄρα χρὼς
ἐτράπετο. Ζεὺς δὲ μεγάλ᾽ ἔκτυπε σήματα φαίνων·

Odyssey 21.405-13

once he had taken up the great bow and looked it all over,
as when a man skilled in the lyre and song
easily stretches the string around a new peg,
fastening the strongly twisted cord of sheep's gut on both sides,
so without any strain Odysseus strung the great bow.
Then plucking it in his right hand he tested the bowstring,
and it gave him back an excellent sound like the voice of a swallow.

---

[3] Translations of the *Iliad* and *Odyssey* are based on those of Lattimore
1951 and 1965, with adjustments. I find the accuracy of his translations a
useful quality here. Other translations, except where noted, are my own; I have
attempted throughout to be very literal for the sake of clarity.
[4] For discussion of Odysseus as poet and the connection of the bow with
song, see Austin 1975.239-53.

A great sorrow fell now upon the suitors, and all their color
was changed, and Zeus showing forth his portents thundered mightily.

This image of Odysseus stringing the bow in the way that
the poet strings the lyre captures the two important elements of
his identity at the moment of vengeance, namely, his identity as
king and poet. His ability to string the bow proves his identity
as the long absent ruler of Ithaca. By his prowess with the bow
he will overcome the suitors and completely reestablish control
as king. That he strings the bow like a poet stringing the lyre
reminds us of the other way in which he has reestablished
himself in Ithaca—his use of the **ainos**. Just as the stringing of
the bow reveals his identity to the suitors, so the image of king
and poet by which he is described reveals Odysseus' two-fold
nature as poet and king.

Odysseus' deception, using the language of epic, is mainly
a verbal one, but, as in drama, there are elements of the visual
as well. He is disguised as a beggar, a disguise that makes him,
in addition to being a poet, an actor. As Orestes will do
throughout the play, Odysseus uses both the deception of
words and of appearance to carry out his plan.[5]

We have another early model of the king as dramatic poet
when, after the killing of the suitors, Odysseus expresses the
fear that the relatives of the suitors will try to avenge their
deaths. He tells Telemachus to create the illusion that there is a
wedding going on in the palace:

αὐτὰρ θεῖος ἀοιδὸς ἔχων φόρμιγγα λίγειαν
ἡμῖν ἡγείσθω φιλοπαίγμονος ὀρχηθμοῖο,
ὥς κέν τις φαίη γάμον ἔμμεναι ἐκτὸς ἀκούων,
ἢ ἀν' ὁδὸν στείχων ἢ οἳ περιναιετάουσι·

Odyssey 23.133-36

---

[5] On Odysseus' use of narrative in the *Odyssey* as a model for its use in
Sophocles' *Philoctetes*, see Roberts 1989.168 and 174.

Then let the inspired singer take his clear-sounding lyre,
and give us the lead for festive dance, so that anyone
who is outside, some one of the neighbors, or a person going
along the street, who hears us, will think we are having a wedding.

At this moment we see Odysseus in the role of director, telling
Telemachus how to use song and dance to create an illusion in
order to deceive his enemies. Similarly, Orestes will direct the
players in his play—first, the Paidagogos and, later, Electra—
telling them how to play their parts.

The figure of Orestes, who, as I shall argue, is being
represented as a poet who brings about **dikê** 'justice' through
his art, has another model in Hesiod. The figure of Hesiod, as
represented in the *Works and Days*, is like both Orestes and
Odysseus, in that he has lost his possessions unjustly. His
brother, Perses, has seized more than his share of the inheritance, and there is no appeal to kings who are corrupt:

ἤδη μὲν γὰρ κλῆρον ἐδασσάμεθ᾽, ἀλλὰ τὰ πολλὰ
ἁρπάζων ἐφόρεις μέγα κυδαίνων βασιλῆας
δωροφάγους, οἳ τήνδε δίκην ἐθέλουσι δίκασσαι.

Works and Days 37-39

For earlier we divided up our inheritance, but
you seized and took away the greater share, greatly glorifying
gift-devouring kings who willingly render this judgment.

There is no external law, no outside authority to which
Hesiod can appeal for restitution. It is only through his art,
through the process of the poem itself, that the poet finally
achieves **dikê**. In the course of the poem we find Perses reduced
to poverty (396) and Hesiod, thus, vindicated.[6] Orestes is like
Hesiod in that there is a family dispute, with his mother and
Aegisthus, over inheritance. For Hesiod, it is the inheritance of

---

[6] For this view of Hesiod, see Nagy 1990a.63-67.

material things; for Orestes, the inheritance of power. Both Hesiod and Orestes find the same means for restoring their rightful share of their father's estate—the power of poetry itself.

In addition to the models of the poet/king in the poetry of epic, we find the same image of poet/lawgiver in the poets Solon and Theognis. Solon is both poet and lawgiver. He gives the Athenians both the poetry that is the ethical foundation of the laws and the code of laws itself. His poetry has the authority of law, and his laws are based on the authority of poetry.[7]

The persona of the poet in Theognis is like Hesiod in that for him, too, **dikê** lies in the poetry itself. He, like Hesiod and Odysseus, has lost his possessions, and waits "for the **dikê** of Zeus to emerge from his own life as dramatized in his own poetry."[8] Theognis is the model of the poet who looks for retribution in life (Theognis 339-40), but who also has a vision of exacting retribution after death (347-48). Hesiod and Solon achieve **dikê** in their own lifetimes, through their own words. In Theognis the poet hopes for the same, but in the poetry itself he has not yet achieved the justice that he longs for.[9]

These patterns apply also to Orestes. He is the dramatic poet who will achieve **dikê** both in his own lifetime and through his own death—the fictitious account of his death that he presents on stage. He achieves, through the poetry of drama, what Theognis hopes to accomplish and what Hesiod and Solon are pictured as actually achieving in wisdom poetry.

With the models of Odysseus, Hesiod, Solon, and Theognis in mind, I would like to examine in detail the opening scene of the play, looking at the authority of Orestes and

---

[7] For this view of Solon, see Nagy 1990a.67-68.
[8] Nagy 1985.71.
[9] For a detailed discussion of Odysseus, Hesiod, Solon, and Theognis in connection with poetry and **dikê**, see Nagy 1985.68-81.

showing that it is the authority of both poet and king. Throughout this scene, and, indeed, the rest of the play, Sophocles is emphasizing speech as the source of Orestes' power. His is the power of words, specifically, the power of poetry. The Paidagogos is presented in terms of an older poet, one who initially has power over the younger poet, Orestes, but who ultimately relinquishes that control. I shall examine the nature of Orestes' authority, its source in words and in his relationship to the Paidagogos, the source of his **paideia** 'education'.[10] This kind of relationship between the older man and the younger can perhaps be seen most clearly in the words of Theognis to Kyrnos:

σοὶ δ᾽ ἐγὼ εὖ φρονέων ὑποθήσομαι οἱάπερ αὐτὸς
Κύρν᾽ ἀπὸ τῶν ἀγαθῶν παῖς ἔτ᾽ ἐὼν ἔμαθον.

Theognis 27-28

But I, with kindly intent, will give you the sort of advice that I myself, Kyrnos, while still a child, learned from good men [**agathoi**].

In this passage the poet sees himself as part of the tradition: he is passing down the tradition, the things he learned from the **agathoi** 'good men' when he was a child. So also the Paidagogos is the **agathos** 'good man' from whom Orestes receives the poetic and ethical tradition.

In this chapter I shall also look at images of light in connection with the power of speech. For Orestes' power is not simply one of words. In addition to the verbal power that he shares with the poets of earlier traditions, he has the dramatic poet's control of the visual. He will use appearances—the way his actors look, the props they carry—to stage successfully the playwright's deception.

---

[10] For the opening scene as one of teacher and student, see Kitzinger 1991.300-304.

I shall consider, too, words of authority and their connection with poetry. In this context I shall include words having to do with engravings and physical impressions, for these images are connected to the **sphragis** 'signet ring' with which Orestes will identify himself to Electra (1222-23). The **sphragis** is not just a seal; it is a small work of art, a beautifully crafted ring. The **sphragis** not only identifies Orestes, but it also identifies the nature of Sophocles' play. It is a small work of art which identifies the play as a work of art about a work of art, a play about play-writing.

This opening scene introduces not only the issues of the authority of the poet and its place in the poetic tradition, but also the idea of the use of deception by the poet and the justification of that use. In Homer, Odysseus is the model of the man who not only uses the deception of poetry, but uses it in a just way. He is the man who uses **ainoi** and the appearance of a beggar—disguises both verbal and visual—to reestablish himself as king of Ithaca. Orestes is an Odyssean figure who uses disguise and deception, the art of the theater, to reestablish **dikê**.

The Paidagogos begins the play by referring to Orestes' relationship to authority:

᾽Ὦ τοῦ <u>στρατηγήσαντος</u> ἐν Τροίᾳ ποτὲ
᾽Αγαμέμνονος παῖ,

Electra 1-2

Son of Agamemnon who once <u>led the army</u> [**stratêgêsantos**] at Troy....[11]

The importance of Orestes' connection with Agamemnon is stressed by the occurrence of the father's name in the very first words of the play. Orestes is the son of the rightful leader of

---

[11] The text of the *Electra* used throughout is based on the 1990 Oxford edition of H. Lloyd-Jones and N. G. Wilson.

Mycenae. The significance of Agamemnon as an authority figure is emphasized immediately with **stratêgêsantos** 'the man who led the army' at Troy. It has been observed of these lines that

> The natural, or prose word-order would be ὦ παῖ Ἀγαμέμνονος τοῦ στρατηγήσαντος [**ô pai Agamemnonos tou stratêgêsantos** 'son of Agamemnon who led the army'].…… The present word-order puts an emphasis on τοῦ στρατηγήσαντος ἐν Τροίᾳ [**tou stratêgêsantos en Troiai** 'who led the army at Troy'] hence upon the fact that Orestes was a young man of brilliant parentage of whom much was to be expected. For the supreme στρατηγία [**stratêgia** 'command'] against Troy was the highest of offices, and the taking of Troy the most famous of military achievements.[12]

The Paidagogos is a double connection for Orestes: he is the link not only to the art of epic poetry, as can be seen later in the messenger speech, but also to the Homeric world itself and to the leader of that world, Orestes' father, Agamemnon.

The Paidagogos first emphasizes the importance of seeing as he continues to speak to the younger man:

> νῦν ἐκεῖν᾽ ἔξεστί σοι
> παρόντι λεύσσειν ὧν πρόθυμος ἦσθ᾽ ἀεί.

Electra 2-3

Now you can see in person
those things you were always eager to see.

As they stand before the palace, the Paidagogos continues to speak, pointing out the landmarks of the plain below (4-8), thus emphasizing the perspective, the view that their return to Agamemnon's home gives them. The Paidagogos, by speaking from a height and indicating what lies below, is already taking

---

[12] Kells 1973 at lines 1ff. of the *Electra*, with transliteration and translation added.

the traditional stance of the prophet and poet who, from a superior vantage point, informs others of what he sees.[13]

That the Paidagogos describes the scene to Orestes also indicates his own relationship to the younger man: he is the man of knowledge and experience, the man who has a sense of tradition and history. And he is the man who transmits the tradition by showing Orestes his place in it.[14]

As he shifts from his description of the plain below to the place where they are standing, the Paidagogos identifies it as Mycenae:

οἳ δ᾽ ἱκάνομεν,
φάσκειν Μυκήνας τὰς πολυχρύσους ὁρᾶν,

Electra 8-9

In this place where we have come, say [**phaskein**]
that you see [**horan**] Mycenae rich in gold [**polukhrusous**]....

Sophocles follows the tradition of Homer and places Agamemnon's home in Mycenae, a choice that contrasts with that of others. Aeschylus in the *Agamemnon* locates it instead in Argos (24), as does Euripides in the *Orestes* (46). The scholion on the *Orestes* passage tells us about the location of Agamemnon's kingdom in the lost works of two other poets, Stesichorus and Simonides, who both place the kingdom in Lacedaemon. Sophocles, with the choice of Mycenae, lets us see his Orestes guided back to a Homeric scene, just as his play points back to its Homeric model. And he emphasizes the Homeric nature of the locale by describing it with the epic epithet **polukhrusous** 'rich in gold'.[15]

---

[13] For this traditional stance of the poet, see Nagy 1989.28.

[14] For a discussion of the, in some ways, similar relationship between Odysseus and Neoptolemos in the *Philoctetes*, see Greengard 1987.

[15] For **polukhrusous** as the epic epithet for Mycenae, see Kamerbeek 1974 on this line and Jebb 1894 on this line, where he cites *Iliad* 7.180 and 11.46, and

In these lines (8-9) the Paidagogos uses the infinitive, **phaskein** 'to say', as an imperative. It is a mild form of order, a suggestion of authority on the part of the Paidagogos. And the order involves words of speaking (**phaskein**) and seeing (**horan** 'to see'). These two words form the beginning and end of the line, framing the Homeric locale, Mycenae, thus drawing attention to themselves and what they frame. The Paidagogos is indicating that he is Orestes' teacher, telling him what to see and what to say. His guidance in things verbal and visual is what he offers the dramatic artist.

The Paidagogos says that Mycenae is the place from which he took Orestes as a child to save him:

ὅθεν σε πατρὸς ἐκ φόνων ἐγώ ποτε
πρὸς σῆς ὁμαίμου καὶ κασιγνήτης λαβὼν
ἤνεγκα κἀξέσωσα κἀξεθρεψάμην
τοσόνδ᾽ ἐς ἥβης πατρὶ τιμωρὸν φόνου.

Electra 11-14

Whence at one time I carried [**ênegka**] you away from your father's bloodshed, taking you from your kinswoman, your sister, and I saved [**kaxesôsa**] you and brought you up [**kaxethrepsamên**] to manhood, as an avenger of your father's murder.

The juxtaposition of the words σε 'you' (referring to Orestes) and πατρός 'father' (11) is another indication of the close identification of the son Orestes with the father Agamemnon and the importance of this identification in the Paidagogos' mind. In addition to the relationship of father to son, the Paidagogos stresses, too, the relationship between Orestes and himself. The Paidagogos emphasizes this relationship of dependence and nurture with three verbs, saying that he was the one who 'took' [**ênegka**] Orestes from Mycenae and 'saved' [**kaxesôsa**] him

---

Odyssey 3.305. For more on this epithet and other Homeric elements in the prologue, see Davidson 1989.59-60.

and 'brought him up' [**kaxethrepsamên**]. That these three verbs together constitute one line makes the statement a forceful one. Moreover, the arrangement of the sounds of the words within this one line also stresses the significance of the the Paidagogos' thought. There is first the repetition of **kax**, in which the **ek** 'out' preverb, emphatic in itself, is repeated in crasis with **kai** 'and'—**kaxesôsa kaxethrepsamên**. The emphatic **ek** is combined with the emphatic repetition of **kai** in one syllable. This combination **kax** is repeated as the last unit of succeeding iambic pairs, stressing in the rhythm of the words themselves the importance of the relationship between Orestes and the Paidagogos.[16] Orestes owes his life and his upbringing to the Paidagogos, as the younger poet owes his artistic life to the earlier poets who developed and transmitted the poetic tradition.

The Paidagogos has not only saved Orestes' life and preserved his sense of tradition; he has given him a purpose, to be the avenger of his father's death (14). The Paidagogos has given him life and a sense of the past in order for him to restore that past, namely, the presence of rightful rule in Mycenae.

The Paidagogos then turns from the past to the matter at hand:

νῦν οὖν, Ὀρέστα καὶ σύ, φίλτατε ξένων
Πυλάδη, τί χρὴ δρᾶν ἐν τάχει βουλευτέον·

Electra 15-16

Now then, Orestes and you, dearest of friends
Pylades, you must plan quickly what to do [**dran**].

---

[16] On the level of semantics only, other critics also see this line as an indication of the Paidagogos' significance in Orestes' life: cf. Kells 1973 at line 13 of the *Electra*, "the accumulation of verbs emphasises the Paedagogus' services to Orestes in rearing him etc. and his consequent dominance over Orestes' ideas and purposes." Cf. Kamerbeek 1974 at line 13 of the *Electra*.

The Paidagogos shows here that he is the person in charge; he is the one who calls the younger men to action. Significantly, the verb he uses for their actions in the play, for the deception that they will carry out, is **dran** 'to do', which is related to the word **drama** 'drama' itself.[17]

The Paidagogos says that they must get on with making their plans since it is already dawn. Even in his urgency, the Paidagogos takes time to describe the dawn, emphasizing both the light and sounds of early morning:

ὡς ἡμὶν ἤδη λαμπρὸν ἡλίου σέλας
ἑῷα κινεῖ φθέγματ᾽ ὀρνίθων σαφῆ
μέλαινά τ᾽ ἄστρων ἐκλέλοιπεν εὐφρόνη.

Electra 17-19

Already for us the bright [lampron] light [selas] of the sun [hêliou]
rouses the clear, early morning [heôia] voices of birds
and the dark night of stars has gone.

Just as the day's agenda at the Athenian dramatic festival itself began at dawn,[18] so the action of Orestes' drama begins in the early morning. The Paidagogos describes the moment not only in terms of light, but also in terms of sound. It is the bright light of the sun that rouses the clear voices of birds. Four words in a row—**lampron** 'bright', **hêliou** 'sun', **selas** 'light', **heôia** 'early morning'—emphasize the radiance of dawn, the light that activates the song of the birds (18). The Paidagogos draws the audience's attention to the importance of light and its association with music, for what he describes now as the circumstances (the light and sound) of their actions (**dran** 16), will be the actions themselves, as Orestes produces a creation of sight and sound, a dramatic spectacle (**theatron** 'theater' from **theaomai** 'see'), to reclaim the rule of Mycenae.

---

[17] Burkert 1985.5; Nagy 1990b.387-88.
[18] Pickard-Cambridge 1968.67.

The Paidagogos draws attention to the beauty of the music and light of early morning because these two elements, sound and sight, are the source of Orestes' power and success. Throughout the play, Orestes will use the music of poetry and the illusions of the stage to regain control in Mycenae. Later in the play, at the moment when Orestes reveals his identity to Electra, her immediate response, her response of recognition, is to address him as the source of light and speech:

Ηλ.   ὦ φίλτατον φῶς. Op. φίλτατον, ξυμμαρτυρῶ.
Ηλ.   ὦ φθέγμ', ἀφίκου; Op. μηκέτ' ἄλλοθεν πύθῃ.

Electra 1224-25

El.   O dearest light. Or. Dearest, I join in the act of being witness.
El.   O voice, have you come? Or. No longer learn from any other source.

The Paidagogos continues to address Orestes, again ordering in a mild way:

πρὶν οὖν τιν' ἀνδρῶν ἐξοδοιπορεῖν στέγης
ξυνάπτετον λόγοισιν·

Electra 20-21

Before anyone comes out of the house
join together [xunapteton] in words [logoisin].

The Paidagogos is directing the two young men: he is their stage-director, showing that he, for now, is the one in charge. The word he uses to order them to join together, **xunapteton** from the verb **sun**'together'-**haptô** 'join', has special significance. One way to read this word is to take it as being used absolutely, in the sense of 'fix together, i.e., arrange (matters).'[19] Reading **xunapteton** in this way means that **logoisin** 'words' is used as an instrumental dative, and the two words together mean 'arrange matters by means of words'.

---

[19] Kells 1973 at line 21 of the *Electra*.

This verb can also be used, as in Herodotus, to mean 'to engage in battle', both with the word **makhê** 'battle' and without (6.108.5 and 4.80.2). In this sense of 'engaging in battle' the meaning of the phrase **xunapteton logoisin** is 'engage in battle by means of words'. The verb is actually used in this way by the comic poet Aristophanes, describing a battle of words in court:

εἰς τάχος παίει ξυνάπτων στρογγύλοις τοῖς ῥήμασι·

Acharnians 686

Quickly he strikes, engaging [verb **sunaptô**] in battle by means of terse words.

The words **xunapteton logoisin**, then, suggest two ideas: one, the idea of arranging matters (the deception of Clytemnestra and Aegisthus) and the other, the idea of engaging in battle. Both the arranging of the deception and the engaging in battle are to be done 'by means of words' [**logoisin**]. The Paidagogos, in the one phrase **xunapteton logoisin**, identifies Orestes as a man who is using words in a struggle for power.

The verb **sunaptô** 'join together' in its basic sense is also a technical term in music. Here the verb in a participial form is used in the term for conjunct tetrachords, συνημένα τετράχορδα 'joined tetratchords'.[20] The related noun form συναφή is, again, the technical term meaning 'the conjunction of two tetrachords'.[21] Both the noun and verb refer to the arrangement in the correct order of the chords of the lyre. Thus, with his instructions to 'join together with words', the Paidagogos indicates that he sees Orestes and Pylades joined together, by

---

[20] For συνημένα τετράχορδα 'joined tetratchords', see Plutarch, *On the Generation of the Soul in the Timaeus* 1029a.

[21] For συναφή 'the conjunction of two tetrachords', see Plutarch, *On Brotherly Love* 491a.

means of words, into a harmonious relationship in order to overcome Clytemnestra and Aegisthus.

The uncompounded form of the verb, **haptô** 'to fasten or bind', is used in Homer also in a context of music and vengeance. When Odysseus is described at the moment that he strings the bow, he is compared to the singer stringing the lyre:

ὡς ὅτ' ἀνὴρ φόρμιγγος ἐπιστάμενος καὶ ἀοιδῆς
ῥηϊδίως ἐτάνυσσε νέῳ περὶ κόλλοπι χορδήν,
ἅψας ἀμφοτέρωθεν ἐϋστρεφὲς ἔντερον οἰός,
ὣς ἄρ' ἄτερ σπουδῆς τάνυσεν μέγα τόξον 'Οδυσσεύς.

Odyssey 21.406-9

As when a man skilled in the lyre and song
easily stretches the string around a new peg
fastening [verb **haptô**] the strongly twisted cord of sheep's gut on both
sides, so without any strain Odysseus strung the great bow.

At the moment when the images of king and poet are joined together, the word for joining, **haptô**, is used. The word appears in a context of music, kingship, and vengeance.

Similarly, Orestes, in his use of **logoisin** 'words' with the verb **sunaptô** 'join with' associates the use of words with an action that combines the martial and the musical in a quest for revenge. The Paidagogos, in his role as guide to the younger men, tells Orestes to use the harmony (**harmonia**, discussed below) of words in a struggle for power.

In his direction to Orestes and his friend, the Paidagogos, by using the imperative form, **xunapteton**, indicates his own relationship to Orestes, his position of authority. In connection with the idea of Orestes as the younger poet guided by the elder, we might think of the tradition reporting Sophocles' own description of himself as a dramatist, having three periods of development (Plutarch *On Progress in Virtue* 79b).[22] First, his style was like that of Aeschylus, described by the word **ogkos** 'bigness, bulk'. Then he entered into a period characterized by 'painful ingenuity in his own invention', πικρὸν καὶ κατάτεχνον τῆς αὐτοῦ κατασκευῆς. The third stage involved a change 'to the kind of diction which is most expressive of character and best', ἠθικώτατον καὶ βέλτιστον. Thus Sophocles is said to have described his own development as having been initially very influenced by the older poet Aeschylus and then developing away from that style to one more his own. We shall see the same development in this first scene with the Paidagogos and Orestes, as the younger man comes on stage guided by the older man, but then asserts himself and takes control.

With regard to the relationship between poets and their predecessors, it is important to remember that Sophocles was considered the most Homeric of the three great tragedians.[23] Homer was a source of inspiration and guidance, a model for Sophocles, just as for Orestes, the Paidagogos is a guide and link to the Homeric world of Mycenae. Sophocles presents Orestes as a poet figure, accepting at first the guidance and control of the earlier poet and then controlling and using what he has learned from the older poet to achieve his own artistic ends.

Orestes responds to the Paidagogos by telling his plans. He begins by addressing him:

---

[22] For a detailed discussion of this passage, see Bowra 1953.108ff. I use his translations of the terms.

[23] For Sophocles as the most Homeric of the tragedians, see the ancient *Vita* [20], where, in a description of the connections between Sophocles and Homer, Sophocles is said to 'draw on the *Odyssey* in many of his plays' (τὴν Ὀδύσσειαν δ' ἐν πολλοῖς δράμασιν ἀπογράφεται) and is said 'to be the only student of Homer' (μόνον Σοφοκλέα τυγχάνειν Ὁμήρου μαθητήν). For a discussion of both ancient and modern views of Sophocles as Homeric, see Easterling 1984 and Davidson 1989.46-49, who focuses on Homeric elements in Sophocles' *Electra*.

ὦ φίλτατ᾽ ἀνδρῶν προσπόλων, ὥς μοι σαφῆ
σημεῖα φαίνεις ἐσθλὸς εἰς ἡμᾶς γεγώς.

Electra 23-24

O most near and dear [most **philos**] of servants, how you show
[**phainô**] me clear [**saphê**] signs [**sêmeia**], noble [**esthlos**] as you are
with regard to us.

These lines include terms associated with both the poetic and
the martial, appropriate associations for a figure who is both
poet and avenging king. The first word to describe the
Paidagogos is φίλτατος 'most **philos**'. The word **philos** is
traditionally used in both epic and wisdom poetry to identify
those in the audience who, like the poet, are **sophoi** 'wise' and
who, because they share in the **sophia** 'wisdom' of the poet, can
interpret the **ainos** 'allusive utterance' of his poetry.[24] The older
man, who has been Orestes' teacher and who will soon be a
player in Orestes' drama, is the most **philos** to Orestes because
he is the most closely associated with him in his development
as a poet.

The Paidagogos is the most **philos** specifically of ἀνδρῶν
προσπόλων 'men who are servants or attendants'. This man is
now identified as a servant. Soon he will play the crucial role of
messenger in the deception of Clytemnestra and Aegisthus. In
that role he will, as directed by Orestes, deliver an **ainos** to
Clytemnestra, which she, having become the least **philos**, will
not understand.

The Paidagogos, then, is, at this early stage in the play,
characterized as teacher, guide, and servant. He will soon be
seen in his role of messenger, where the audience will see him
display his skill as poet and actor. As such, he fits in many

---

[24] For the use of these terms by poets, with reference to poetic audience, see
Nagy 1979.236-42 and 1985.23-31.

ways Theognis' description of the poet, the attendant and messenger of the Muses:

χρὴ Μουσῶν θεράποντα καὶ ἄγγελον, εἴ τι περισσὸν
εἰδείη, σοφίης μὴ φθονερὸν τελέθειν,
ἀλλὰ τὰ μὲν μῶσθαι, τὰ δὲ δεικνύναι, ἄλλα δὲ ποιεῖν·
τί σφιν χρήσηται μοῦνος ἐπιστάμενος;[25]

Theognis 769-72

The servant and messenger of the Muses must, if he knows anything
extraordinary, not be begrudging of his wisdom,
but must seek out and display some things, and create some others;
what use will it be for him, if he alone understands?

The Paidagogos is characterized as a poet who, like the poet in Theognis, is a servant and messenger, the man who seeks (cf. μῶσθαι) things out (Mycenae, the past), who displays (cf. δεικνύναι) them (the landmarks of Mycenae, the story of Orestes' death), and who creates (cf. ποιεῖν) things (again, the way of telling the story of Orestes' death). He is the one who, because he is the most **philos** (23), is most able to communicate as poet to audience, as audience to poet.

In this same passage, the Paidagogos is recognized not only as the most **philos**, but also as the man who is **esthlos** 'noble' (24). The word **esthlos** is synonymous with **agathos**, the word that characterizes the man who, by virtue of being intrinsically noble, is able to decode the **ainos** of poetry.[26]

Orestes' first lines of address to the Paidagogos have connections not only with the poetic, but also with the martial. One commentator has indicated that **sêmeia phainô** 'to show signs'(24) is an expression used by a general to his men,

---

[25] For a detailed discussion of this passage, see Edmunds 1985.100-109.
[26] For passages illustrating the requirement that one be **philos, sophos,** and **agathos** in order to undestand the **ainos** of the poet, see Nagy 1979.236-42 and 1989.10-11.

translating "O dearest of *men*-servants [italics not mine], what clear directives you issue (lit. 'show') to me, splendid fellow that you are to me," and cites uses of **sêmeia phainô** as a military term.[27] The word **phainô** is also used with regard to sound, in the sense of 'to make clear' to the ear. It is used in this way, in fact, in the description of the Phaeacian poet Demodokos as he begins to sing the tale of the Trojan horse, φαῖνε δ᾽ ἀοιδήν 'he showed his song' (*Odyssey* 8.499). The word **phainô**, then, is connected both with the sound of poetry and the command of a military leader. So too the description of the Paidagogos, in the initial two lines of Orestes' first speech, characterizes him as a man with the nature of both poet and general, a man of words and authority. The Paidagogos, the teacher of Orestes and his model in life, is presented in terms that will soon characterize Orestes himself, the poet and leader who will reestablish **dikê** in Mycenae.

In addition to having associations with sound and authority, the description of the Paidagogos as showing clear **sêmeia** 'signs' could be a description of Orestes himself in the recognition scene with Electra. The word **sêmeion**, as well as meaning 'sign', can also mean 'signet ring', the object with which Orestes will identify himself to Electra (1222-23). According to some interpretations of Orestes' words to the Paidagogos at this earlier point in the play (23-24),[28] Orestes is saying that the Paidagogos shows 'clear signs' that he is an **esthlos** 'noble' or 'genuine man'.[29] In the same way, later in the play, Orestes, like his model the Paidagogos, will show with a clear sign—the signet ring—that he is the genuine man, the real Orestes, the true voice of the community.

---

27 Kells 1973 at line 23 of the *Electra*.
28 Jebb 1894 and Kamerbeek 1974 at lines 23-25 of the *Electra*.
29 For **esthlos** in the sense of 'genuine', see Watkins 1972.555.

Orestes continues to address the Paidagogos, saying that he is like a noble horse who, though old, does not lose courage at the moment of danger (25-6), and then says to the Paidagogos,

ἡμᾶς τ᾽ ὀτρύνεις καὐτὸς ἐν πρώτοις ἕπῃ.

Electra 28

you urge us on and you yourself follow among the first.

Orestes, by identifying the Paidagogos first as one of the πρόσπολοι 'servants' (23) and now by comparing him with a faithful horse, asserts his authority over him. The Paidagogos' role now is to urge the younger men on (ὀτρύνεις)—he is not to lead, but to inspire. This change from leader to follower is emphasized by the last verb in the sentence, ἕπῃ 'you follow'. The Paidagogos is still an important figure, he is 'among the first' (ἐν πρώτοις), but, as the verb ἕπῃ indicates, he is a follower now. This role of follower contrasts to his role during Orestes' youth when the Paidagogos was the man who, by his own description, took the initiative and saved Orestes (13). The Paidagogos was a Phoenix figure in Orestes' childhood, the man who protected and nurtured him and had the control of a parent. Now Orestes, having reached Mycenae and maturity, becomes the authority figure, the man who first exerts control over his earlier protector and teacher and then over the community and leaders of Mycenae itself.

In his next lines Orestes continues to emphasize his position of authority. But he is still somewhat tentative, still looking for the older man's approval and guidance:

τοιγὰρ τὰ μὲν δόξαντα δηλώσω, σὺ δὲ
ὀξεῖαν ἀκοὴν τοῖς ἐμοῖς λόγοις διδούς,
εἰ μή τι καιροῦ τυγχάνω, μεθάρμοσον.

Electra 29-31

I will show you then what I've decided, and you,
giving a keen ear to my words,
<u>correct</u> [**metharmozô**] me, if I am at all off the mark.

Orestes is giving an order, but it is an order to the Paidagogos to correct him, **metharmozô**. Orestes, while assuming his role as leader, still recognizes and respects the knowledge and experience of the older man. We note also that as Orestes asks for advice, the emphasis is on hearing, ὀξεῖαν ἀκοήν 'a keen ear' (30). The importance of hearing and of sound was first suggested by the comparison between the Paidagogos and the old horse pricking up its ears (27). Sound and the need to listen are now emphasized again in Orestes' order. By listening keenly the Paidagogos will be able to correct Orestes.

The verb **metharmozô** comes in a position of prominence as the word that both ends the line and the sentence. It is used in this emphatic position, in a context of hearing and command, because it is a word that in and of itself connects sound, specifically, the sound of music and poetry, with authority.

We see this connection between poetry and authority by looking more closely at the verb and related words. The word **metharmozô** is a technical term in music for changing the mode.[30] This change entails a re-tuning of the lyre. When Orestes uses the word here, he is asking that the Paidagogos re-tune his words in the way that one re-tunes the strings of the lyre.

We find the uncompounded form of this verb, **harmozô**, and the related noun **harmonia** used with respect to music and government. The two words come from the verb root *ar- 'fit together', as in ἀραρίσκω 'fit, join'.[31] The noun **harmonia** is a

---

[30] Iamblichus *On the Life of Pythagoras* 25.113.
[31] For this derivation and the following discussion of **harmonia** as conveying both musical and social cohesion, see Nagy 1979.297-300, 1985.27-29, and 1990b.91-101.

musical term, the equivalent of 'tuning' more than of the current sense of 'harmony'. The verb **harmozô**, in addition to being used for 'tuning' instruments,[32] is used as a word connected to authority. In this sense it is found in the Spartan constitution where **harmozô** means 'act as **harmostês** (ἁρμοστής)'.[33] The **harmostês** was the governor sent out by the Spartans to subject cities.[34]

When Orestes orders the Paidagogos to listen intently to his words and to correct him, he is using the verb **metharmozô** with both its musical and political associations. He is asking the Paidagogos to 'act as **harmostês**', to be the governor and corrector of his words. He is also asking him to help him join his words together in a 'well-tuned' way. The choice of the word **metharmozô** indicates the importance of the use of harmony of words, the use of poetry, in the attempt to regain control of Mycenae.

By using the verb **metharmozô** in its meaning of 'to correct, to be **harmostês**', Orestes recognizes the Paidagogos as an authority figure, a corrector. But the use of the verb as an imperative, an order, indicates that Orestes is beginning to control the corrector, the Paidagogos. Orestes is taking control while still recognizing the authority of his old and valued teacher.

As his opening speech continues, Orestes next identifies the authority for his taking vengeance by means of deception. That source of authority is the god of poetry and prophecy, Apollo himself:

---

[32] Plato *Philebus* 56a, where the verb occurs in its Attic form ἁρμόττω.
[33] Xenophon *Respublica Lacedaemoniorum* 14.2.
[34] Thucydides 8.5; Xenophon *Hellenica* 2.4.28. Kells 1973 on these lines says that **metharmozô** "again recalls Orestes' liking for discipline, especially of the Spartan variety" and makes the connection between this verb and the noun **harmostês**.

28   *Chapter 1*

ἐγὼ γὰρ ἡνίχ᾽ ἱκόμην τὸ Πυθικὸν
μαντεῖον, ὡς μάθοιμ᾽ ὅτῳ τρόπῳ πατρὶ
δίκας ἀροίμην τῶν φονευσάντων πάρα,
χρῆ μοι τοιαῦθ᾽ ὁ Φοῖβος ὧν πεύσῃ τάχα·
ἄσκευον αὐτὸν ἀσπίδων τε καὶ στρατοῦ
δόλοισι κλέψαι χειρὸς ἐνδίκου σφαγάς.

Electra 32-37

For when I came to the Pythian
oracle to learn how
I might exact vengeance for my father from his murderers,
Phoebus proclaimed to me things which you will quickly learn:
that I myself, without shields and army, by means of
deceptions [**doloi**] should stealthily carry out the slaying of a just hand.

Apollo is the original authority for the killing of
Clytemnestra and Aegisthus, and he is the one who instructs
Orestes to use **doloi** 'deceptions' in order to accomplish his
ends. Orestes looks beyond the authority of the Paidagogos to
the authority of the god Apollo. Just as the Paidagogos as poet
is a model and inspiration for the younger artist, so Apollo, the
god of poetry, is a source of inspiration. He is the one who
inspires Orestes to face his enemies armed only with **doloi**, and
he is the one who instructs Orestes to use these **doloi**, which
will be the deceptions of the theater, to accomplish vengeance.

Apollo's role as the inspiration and authority for the use
of deception is similar to that of Athena in the *Odyssey*.[35] The
use of disguise is part of Athena's instructions to Odysseus as
the hero and goddess plan his return to Ithaca (*Odyssey* 13.392-
415). Athena is the author of Odysseus' use of deception to
regain his power, as Apollo is the author of Orestes'. The
parallel of the god advising the use of deception suggests again

[35] See Davidson 1989.54.

the identification of Orestes with the poet/king figure Odysseus.

Orestes goes on to describe the deception, first indicating his authority over the Paidagogos by ordering him to learn everything that is going on inside the house (40). He then speaks about the visual aspects of the deception, the fact that because of the Paidagogos' age, the fact that he is much older than when he left Mycenae, no one in the house will suspect the Paidagogos of being who he is (42-3). After this visual aspect of the deception, he introduces the verbal aspect in the next line:

λόγῳ δὲ χρῶ τοιῷδ', ὅτι ξένος μὲν εἶ

Electra 44

Use this <u>story</u> [logos], that you are a stranger....

Here is the beginning of Orestes' telling the player how to play his part.[36] It begins with an order, χρῶ 'use', as Orestes acts as director. What he tells the actor to use is **logos**, the word that means 'speech' in general, and 'story' in specific. Orestes is here emphasizing the need for speech to achieve the deception. Thus, as Orestes begins to describe the drama that he and the Paidagogos are about to produce, we find references to both the visual (the appearance of the aged man) and the verbal (the story) aspects of the deception.

Orestes tells the Paidagogos how to play his part as the messenger telling the story of Orestes' supposed death to Clytemnestra:

ἄγγελλε δ' ὅρκον προστιθεὶς ὁθούνεκα
τέθνηκ' Ὀρέστης ἐξ ἀναγκαίας τύχης,

Electra 47-48

---

[36] Similar to Odysseus' directing Neoptolemos in the opening of the *Philoctetes*.

Announce, adding an oath [**horkos**], that
Orestes has died from a fatal accident....

Commentators have generally had difficulty with the word
horkos 'oath' here.[37] Among other objections is the fact that the
Paidagogos never does give an oath when he tells Clytemnestra
the story later. The emendation ὄγκον from **ogkos** 'bulk' has
been suggested, with ὄγκον προστιθείς meaning 'adding bulk (to
my sketch)'.[38] With this emendation Orestes is describing the
elaborate style that he wishes the Paidagogos to use in the
messenger speech. With the word **ogkos**, Orestes is describing
that style in the same way that Sophocles is said to have
described the earliest stage of his own style, the one during
which he was most influenced by the older dramatist
Aeschylus.[39]

Using the word **ogkos** Orestes directs the Paidagogos to
tell the story in the padded style, in the ornamented style of
earlier poets.[40] Like Sophocles, Orestes will start out by using
the style of his predecessors in a context of his own. The
Paidagogos' later speech about the death of Orestes in the
chariot race is the most Homeric speech in the play. As one
commentator remarks with regard to **ogkos** here, " 'Bulk' (or
'padding') is just what the Paedagogus does add, when he
comes to tell his story."[41] Orestes, as he continues with his brief
summary of the story of his death that the Paidagogos is to tell,
uses an ornamental epithet, τροχήλατος 'wheel-drawn' (49), to
describe the chariot from which he is supposedly hurled and, as
this same critic notes, with this epithet, "the idea of

---

[37] Among them are Jebb 1894, Kells 1973, and Kamerbeek 1974.
[38] Kells 1973 suggests this emendation by Musgrave.
[39] For discussion, see pp. 20-21 above.
[40] The word **ogkos** is used of a 'lofty style' by Aristotle (ὄγκος τῆς λέξεως *Rhetoric* 1407b26), and of the 'fullness and breadth of epic poetry' (ὁ τοῦ ποιήματος ὄγκος *Poetics* 1459b28).
[41] Kells 1973 at line 47 of the *Electra*.

ornamenting, expanding the story of Orestes' death in a chariot-race, is already hinted at."[42]

Looking further at Orestes' summary of the story of his death (47-50), we see Orestes acting like the director of a play who instructs a player by acting out the part. As another commentator points out,

> The tone and the wording are such that Orestes strikes us as enacting for a moment the part the old man is asked to play. τέθνηκ' 'Ορέστης ['he has died, Orestes'], pathetic by its emphatic word order, is echoed *infra* 673, ἐξ ἀναγκαίας τύχης ['from a fatal accident'] is an impressive formula for his fate (cf. *Ajax* 485, 803) and ἐκ τροχηλάτων δίφρων κυλισθείς ['hurled from the wheel-drawn chariot'] has the perfect ring of messengers' rhetoric.[43]

Orestes concludes his summary of the Paidagogos' messenger speech with the words ὧδ' ὁ μῦθος ἐστάτω 'let the story [muthos] be established to this effect' (50). Orestes asserts the authority of his story and its power, using an imperative form of the verb ἵστημι 'to set up, establish'. Later, when Electra is speaking to her sister, we shall find that someone else has already 'established' her own form of drama in Mycenae. Electra says of her mother:

εὑροῦσ' ἐκείνην ἡμέραν ἐν ᾗ τότε
πατέρα τὸν ἀμὸν ἐκ δόλου κατέκτανεν,
ταύτῃ χοροὺς ἵστησι....

Electra 278-80

having found the day on which she
killed my father by treachery,
on that day she establishes a chorus [khorous histêsi]....

---

42 Kells 1973 at line 49 of the *Electra*.
43 Kamerbeek 1974 at lines 48-50 of the *Electra*.

The term **khorous histêsi** is the regular term for instituting a chorus.[44] It is the way to describe what the poet does and from it comes the name Stesichorus, Στησίχορος, 'he who sets up the chorus'.[45] Clytemnestra has set up a chorus that celebrates the death of Agamemnon, thus establishing his death as a good thing, a cause for rejoicing. Orestes intends to establish his own **muthos** 'story', by which he will avenge his father's death and thus invalidate Clytemnestra's chorus. Orestes will prove that his fiction has more power than Clytemnestra's.

Orestes then says that they will take offerings to his father's tomb (51-53) and return:

εἶτ᾽ ἄψορρον ἥξομεν πάλιν,
τύπωμα χαλκόπλευρον ἡρμένοι χεροῖν,

Electra 53-54

then we shall come back again
bearing a bronze-sided <u>casting</u> [**tupôma**] in our hands....

The bronze casting, or urn, which will appear to hold the ashes of Orestes' body, will be the major prop of the play that Orestes will stage for Clytemnestra. Significantly, Orestes does not use an ordinary word for 'urn' here, such as λέβης, which Aeschylus uses in the *Choephoroe* (686). Instead, he refers to the urn as a **tupôma** 'casting' that is χαλκόπλευρον 'bronze-sided'.

The word **tupôma** for the urn distinguishes it as an object related to the **sphragis** 'seal, signet ring'. The word **tupôma** is used of anything formed or molded. It is related to the verb **tuptô** 'strike, beat' and to the noun **tupos** 'blow' or 'the effect of a blow or pressure'. The word **tupos**, in this second sense of 'something struck', comes to be the word for the impression of a

---

[44] Jebb 1894 at lines 280f of the *Electra* who cites Demosthenes *Against Meidias* 21.51.
[45] Calame I 1977.88-9n91 and 61n23 and Nagy 1990b.361-62.

seal,[46] and so, like the **sphragis** itself, it is a work of art that indicates the identity and authority of the one who uses it.

The word **tupos** is associated with other works of art besides seals. It is used of any figure worked in relief.[47] In this way it comes to mean 'image'[48] and is even used of children as 'images' of their parents.[49] As we shall see in this play, the seal, the signet ring, is what connects Orestes with his father and identifies him as his son.

The word **tupos** can also mean 'archetype, model', and from this sense it comes to mean a 'model to be imitated'. In Plato's *Republic*, **tupoi** are models of behavior which men must imitate or avoid imitating.[50] The word **tupoi** is used in the sense of 'patterns' on which the poets must model their stories and from which they may not deviate:

οἰκισταῖς δὲ τοὺς μὲν τύπους προσήκει εἰδέναι ἐν οἷς δεῖ μυθολογεῖν τοὺς ποιητάς, παρ'οὓς ἐὰν ποιῶσιν οὐκ ἐπιτρεπτέον....

Republic 379a

It is fitting for the founders to know models [tupoi] on which the poets should base their stories; if they create stories contrary to these, it is not acceptable....

In this sense of having a model for a story, the word **tupos** reminds us of poets using the works of earlier artists as models for their own, as Sophocles used Homer, as Orestes uses the Paidagogos.

---

[46] Euripides *Hippolytus* 876; Plato *Theaetetus* 192a and 194b and *Republic* 377b.

[47] Herodotus 2.106.2, 136.1, 138.2, 148.7, 153.1.

[48] Herodotus 2.86.7, 3.88.4.

[49] Artemidorus Daldianus 2.45.

[50] See Plato *Republic* 396e, a discussion of what models the guardians must avoid in their youth, and 396b, a discussion of what models the virtuous man avoids in narration.

The word **tupôma**, then, in its connection with **tupos**, has associations both with art—the **sphragis** and other figures in relief—and with the authority of archetypes and models. With its connections to art and authority, it appears in the *Electra* in a context of deception. Orestes has just said that he and the Paidagogos, after making their offerings at Agamemnon's tomb,

> εἶτ' ἄψορρον ἥξομεν πάλιν,
> <u>τύπωμα</u> χαλκόπλευρον ἠρμένοι χεροῖν,
> ὃ καὶ σὺ θάμνοις οἶσθά που κεκρυμμένον,
> ὅπως λόγῳ κλέπτοντες ἡδεῖαν φάτιν
> φέρωμεν αὐτοῖς, τοὐμὸν ὡς ἔρρει δέμας
> φλογιστὸν ἤδη καὶ κατηνθρακωμένον.

Electra 53-58

> then we shall come back again,
> bearing a bronze-sided <u>casting</u> [**tupôma**] in our hands,
> which you know is hidden somewhere in the bushes,
> so that, deceiving them with speech, we may bring them
> a welcome story: that now my body has perished
> in flame and burned to ash.

The urn is hidden, κεκρυμμένον, and it is the prop which will help in the deception that they are preparing for Clytemnestra and Aegisthus, λόγῳ κλέπτοντες 'deceiving them with speech'.

The word **tupôma**, then, connected with seals of authority, archetypes, models to be imitated, and works of art, is used of the object which will be a major prop in the deception that Orestes intends to execute. Hence, we have a word of authenticity and art in a context of deception, an early suggestion in the play of the use of deception in art to establish authority.

One critic, considering the associations of the urn with deception, sees the urn as a work of art which is a symbol for the play itself:

In its close associations with speech and action, falsehood and truth, the urn also functions as a symbol of the deception of the theatrical situation *per se*. In this respect it is ... a "metatragic" symbol of tragedy calling attention to its own medium as a literary fiction and as a set of conventions of language, action, music, dance.... It is a work of art and elaborate artifice (cf. [**t u p ô m a khalkopleuron**], 54) which gathers around itself the power of language to deceive or to establish truth. It functions, then, as a symbol of the play itself, a work whose falsehood (fiction) embodies truth.[51]

The urn and the **sphragis**, both works of art, are the two major props of the play. The urn is the prop used to disguise Orestes' identity; the **sphragis** is the one to reveal it. The play is about art that, like the urn, deceives, and, like the **sphragis**, reveals the truth. The urn is made from being impressed with something from without; it receives an impression. The **sphragis** is something that gives an impression. The urn is like the play itself, a work of art shaped and created by an outside force, a **sphragis**. That outside force, the **sphragis**, is the power and authority of the poet, who shapes the play in a way that identifies it as distinctly his own.

Orestes comments on his use of the deceptive story of his death:

τί γάρ με λυπεῖ τοῦθ', ὅταν λόγῳ θανὼν
ἔργοισι σωθῶ κἀξενέγκωμαι <u>κλέος</u>;
δοκῶ μέν, οὐδὲν ῥῆμα σὺν <u>κέρδει</u> κακόν.
ἤδη γὰρ εἶδον πολλάκις καὶ τοὺς <u>σοφοὺς</u>
λόγῳ μάτην θνῄσκοντας· εἶθ', ὅταν δόμους
ἔλθωσιν αὖθις, ἐκτετίμηνται πλέον·
ὡς κἄμ' ἐπαυχῶ τῆσδε τῆς φήμης ἄπο
δεδορκότ' ἐχθροῖς ἄστρον ὣς λάμψειν ἔτι.

Electra 59-66

[51] Segal 1980/81.136.

For what does it grieve me, when, dying in word,
I am saved by deeds and gain glory [**kleos**]?
I think that no word, with profit [**kerdos**], is bad.
For often already I have seen even wise [**sophoi**] men
falsely die in story; then, when they come home
again, they have been honored all the more.
So I am confident that from this story I,
alive, shall yet shine upon my enemies like a star.

Here we have the emphasis on the deception of words and the use of this deception by the poet. Dying in word, λόγῳ θανών (59), Orestes will be saved and will gain **kleos** 'glory'. The word **kleos** means not simply 'glory', the good fame that Orestes will receive for avenging his father's death, but etymologically, as the noun related to κλύω 'hear', the word **kleos** has the original meaning 'that which is heard'. It is the word for the 'glory' conferred by the 'hearing of poetry'.[52] Orestes says that by creating the fictitious account of his death and having it presented by the Paidagogos, thus, by creating a play, he will gain **kleos** 'the glory conferred by poetry'. Orestes is assuming the role of the poet who traditionally controls **kleos**: "In a word, the Hellenic poet is the master of **kleos**."[53] Orestes will be not only the giver, but also the receiver of his own **kleos**. Traditionally, poets, in return for the praise and **kleos** which their poetry gave others, gained their own **kleos** by virtue of being the composers of the poetry. Orestes, however, will have not simply the **kleos** which the poetry confers; he will have the **kleos** of the poet who confers it. His will be the double **kleos** of both the giver and the receiver.

In these lines, too, Orestes presents his view of the relationship of words and deeds, as he describes the play that he and the Paidagogos are about to create and perform. By 'dying

---

[52] Nagy 1979.16n3. For a more detailed discussion, see Nagy 1974.231-55.
[53] Nagy 1979.16.

in word', λόγῳ θανών (59), that is, by creating a fictitious account of his death, Orestes expects to be saved by 'actions', ἔργοισι (60), and to 'gain the glory that is gained through the hearing of poetry', κἀξενέγκωμαι κλέος (60). Orestes is not making, as some have thought,[54] the traditional contrast between 'word' and 'deed'. For the 'deeds' by which Orestes will be saved are the 'deeds' that constitute the performance of the play—the verbal and visual deception created to deceive Clytemnestra and Aegisthus. The 'actions' include the act of speaking.[55] What may appear initially as a contrast between word and deed is in fact the identification of one with the other. Later in the play, Electra will complain that Orestes keeps saying that he will return, but never does (169-72; 319). His words are separate from action and are powerless. However, when he returns to Mycenae, his words do not simply match his actions; his words become part of the action itself. He creates a play and the play is the joining of words and action. His words are powerful when they are acted out in the context of the play.

In this same passage Orestes also justifies the use of deception, the deception of poetry, οὐδὲν ῥῆμα σὺν κέρδει κακόν 'no word, with **kerdos** 'profit', is bad' (61). Again, Orestes is like Homer's Odysseus, the model of the poet/king, who creates his own drama to deceive. Odysseus, after the death of the suitors, orders the singer and dancers to pretend that a

---

[54] Among commentators, see Kells 1973 at line 15 and Kamerbeek 1974 at line 60 of the *Electra*.

[55] For discussion of the concept of the speech-act, see Austin 1962 and Searle 1979. For examples of discussion of the whole play in terms of **logos** 'word' and **ergon** 'deed', see Woodard 1964.163-205, who sees the play as one that recognizes and ultimately heals a breach between **logos** and **ergon**; for another example, see Minadeo 1967.114-42, who reads the play as one that first establishes the futility of the **logos** and then shows a progression from **logos** to **ergon**. For discussion of false words that are actions in Sophocles' *Philoctetes*, see Taplin 1987.71-72.

wedding is going on so that no one will suspect that the suitors have been killed (*Odyssey* 23.130-40). This performance will allow Odysseus to go to his estate and to see

ὅττι κε κέρδος 'Ολύμπιος ἐγγυαλίξῃ.

Odyssey 23.140

what profit [kerdos] the Olympian puts in our hands.

This deception will allow Odysseus to find out what **kerdos** Zeus offers him. Here we have Odysseus acting as a dramatist, as it were, arranging a deception that concerns murder for revenge, and this dramatic deception is associated with **kerdos** in its positive aspect, a **kerdos** from Zeus. This connection between the artist's use of deception and the **kerdos** that such a deception brings is the same in the case of Orestes. Orestes sees the deception of the theater as a means of gaining **kerdos** in its most positive aspect.

The word **kerdos** does not simply mean 'gain'. The word, cognate with Old Irish *cerd* 'craft', can mean simply the 'craft' of poetry.[56] Orestes is saying that no word, when it is used in an artistic way, with **kerdos**, is base. He is justifying the artist's use of deception.

Orestes says that he has often seen the **sophoi** 'wise' die falsely in story, but when they return home they have been honored all the more (62-64). We have seen that the word **sophoi** is used to describe those skilled in poetry.[57] This idea of the **sophos** 'wise man' who dies in story and returns home has to call to mind the most famous story of the return of a **sophos**, the story of Odysseus.[58] Parallel stories in Herodotus also have

[56] Nagy 1989.19 and 1990b.56-57
[57] See p. 22 above.
[58] Kamerbeek 1974 cites the scholion to lines 62-64, which suggests Pythagoras and Odysseus as possible references. Jebb 1894 says that there cannot be a reference to Odysseus here: "as Odysseus did not contrive the

been suggested as references, including the stories of Salmoxis (Herodotus 4.95.1-5) and Aristeas of Proconnesus (4.14.1-3).[59]

According to Herodotus, Salmoxis wished to make the Thracians believe in the doctrine of immortality. He built an underground chamber and disappeared into it, thus deceiving them into thinking that he was dead. In the fourth year after his disappearance, he reappeared and in this way convinced the Thracians that what he had taught about immortality was true. Salmoxis is like a playwright—he staged his own death and reappearance. Like Orestes, he used dramatic deception to establish his authority in the community.

Aristeas, in Herodotus' account, was a poet, a native of the island of Marmora, who was reported to have died. Seven years after the report of his death, however, he returned home. When he came back, he composed the poem (ποιῆσαι τὰ ἔπεα) that Herodotus cites as a source of information about the Issedones. Herodotus uses Aristeas, the poet, as an authority for his narrative.

Orestes is using the word **sophos** (62) because it is the word that describes the poet. It calls to mind the stories of other poet-like figures, Odysseus, Salmoxis, and Aristeas, who once disappeared, but returned to become authority figures in the community. Like Aristeas, who used words, like Salmoxis, who used illusion, like Odysseus, who used both, Orestes is returning to establish himself as the authority in Mycenae. He, too, will use poetry and illusion to regain control in the community.

Orestes concludes his vision of success:

---

rumor of his own death, the case is not in point." But Orestes is talking in general about men who have died in stories; he has not restricted his comments to men who have told the story themselves. For further discussion, see Davidson 1989.57-58.

[59] Jebb 1894 and Kamerbeek 1974 at lines 62-64 of the *Electra*, and Segal 1981.252.

ὡς κἄμ᾽ ἐπαυχῶ τῆσδε τῆς φήμης ἄπο
δεδορκότ᾽ ἐχθροῖς ἄστρον ὡς λάμψειν ἔτι.

Electra 65-66

So I am confident that from this story I,
alive, shall yet shine upon my enemies like a star.

Orestes describes his success in the dramatist's terms, in terms
of sound and sight, of word and spectacle. He says that he is
confident, ἐπαυχῶ 'I boast', using a word that draws attention
to the fact that he is speaking. He uses a word of sight,
δεδορκότα, to describe himself as 'alive'. It is from its basic
meaning 'to see' that the verb δέρκομαι comes to mean 'to be
alive'.

Orestes describes himself as a star that will shine, and the
very word for 'shine' is one which is used not only of light, but
also of sounds that 'ring out' (παιὰν δὲ λάμπει 'the hymn to
Apollo rings out' Sophocles *Oedipus Tyrannus* 186; λάμπει κλέος
'kleos rings out' Pindar *Olympian* 1.23). His ultimate vision of
himself is one of light that has its source in words: he will be
like a star (ἄστρον) that will shine (λάμψειν) as a result of
words that have been spoken (τῆς φήμης ἄπο). This description
of something visual that has its source in words is a description
of drama itself, for drama not only has its foundation in the
earlier traditions of poetry, its verbal source, but has, in
addition, the radiance of the visual, the spectacle (**theatron**
'theater' is derived from the verb **theaomai** 'see') that emerges
from the poetry.

The idea of drama as a medium not only of words, but of
sight, brings us back to the Paidagogos' original command to
Orestes, **xunapteton logoisin** 'join together in words' (21). The
verb **xunapteton**, as discussed above, comes from the verb
haptô, meaning 'to join together'.[60] In addition, the verb also

[60] See pp. 18-20 above.

means 'to set on fire'. Orestes sees himself appearing in his play first, not as a man, but as the contents of the urn, the body that has been burned and reduced to ash, φλογιστὸν ἤδη καὶ κατηνθρακωμένον (58). From this ash he will emerge living, radiant, like a shining star. So, too, later in the play, in Clytemnestra's prophetic dream, when Agamemnon returns to life, he is pictured on the hearth coming back into the light (ἐλθόντος εἰς φῶς 419). Both father and son are pictured rising from the the ashes to light and life. Through the medium of the play, a medium both of word and vision, the son, and the father through him, will return to the light.

With the word **xunapteton** the Paidagogos captures both the idea of the verbal and the visual in drama. The Paidagogos is telling the young men both to put things together with words and to set things aflame, to use the power both of words and of light, the verbal and the visual that are the two-fold source of the force of drama.

Orestes ends his first speech of the play with a prayer for success (67-72) and then directs the three men off stage:

σοὶ δ' ἤδη, γέρον,
τὸ σὸν μελέσθω βάντι φρουρῆσαι χρέος·
νὼ δ' ἔξιμεν· καιρὸς γάρ, ὅσπερ ἀνδράσι
μέγιστος ἔργου παντός ἐστ' ἐπιστάτης.

Electra 73-76

You, now, old man,
take care that you go and see to your task.
The two of us shall exit; for here is the critical moment, which for men
is, in every deed, the greatest overseer.

Orestes is in command of the situation. Like the playwright, he watches the pacing and controls the exit of characters off stage. But as the three men prepare to exit, the sound of a voice stops them:

ἰώ μοί μοι δύστηνος.

Electra 77

Alas for me, wretched one.

The Electra of Sophocles' play, unlike the Electra of Aeschylus (*Choephoroe* 16-18) and Euripides (*Electra* 107), is heard before she is seen on stage, because the voice, the poetic voice, is what has significance and power in Sophocles' play. Before hearing Electra, Orestes was in command of the situation. Now Electra's line, in a lyric meter that intensifies her words and contrasts with Orestes' iambic lines of ordinary dialogue, has power over him. When the Paidagogos notes the sound of Electra's voice (78-79), Orestes is at a loss as to what to do:

ἆρ' ἐστὶν ἡ δύστηνος Ἠλέκτρα; θέλεις
μείνωμεν αὐτοῦ κἀνακούσωμεν γόων;

Electra 80-81[61]

Is it Electra, the wretched one? Do you wish
us to stay here and listen to her cries?

Instead of directing the Paidagogos to exit, Orestes now looks to him to take charge, to decide whether they should stay and listen to Electra.[62] The Paidagogos assumes command, telling him that they must not stay:

ἥκιστα· μηδὲν πρόσθεν ἢ τὰ Λοξίου
πειρώμεθ' ἔρδειν, κἀπὸ τῶνδ' ἀρχηγετεῖν,

---

[61] For these lines as properly attributed to Orestes and for remarks on the Paidagogos' role as parallel to that of Eumaeus and Philoetius in the *Odyssey*, see Lloyd-Jones and Wilson 1990b.44.

[62] Even in his distress Orestes is still the natural poet, incorporating the work of others into his own. He takes a word from Electra's lyric line, δύστηνος 'wretched' (77), and uses it in the context of his own iambic meter (80).

πατρὸς χέοντες λουτρά· ταῦτα γὰρ φέρειν
νίκην τέ φημι καὶ κράτος τῶν δρωμένων.

Electra 82-85

Not at all; let us attempt to do nothing before
the things of Loxias, and from there let us attempt to begin,
pouring the libations of your father; for these things, I declare,
bring victory and power over the things being done.

Orestes had asked not whether they should stay to speak with Electra, but whether they should stay to listen to her (81). The Paidagogos takes charge by brusquely dismissing the suggestion, ἥκιστα 'Not at all' (82). In effect, he is depriving Electra of her audience. As the play develops, we shall see that the play itself is a competition of voices. Each player—Clytemnestra, Electra, Chrysothemis, Aegisthus—will insist on different versions of the past, different stories that justify their actions in the present. Each will try to establish as true his or her own version of the past. Orestes' triumph will be to establish his version of the story—the play which he presents—as the one with power and authority.

Here we see the Paidagogos not only in his role as poet/playwright, but as teacher and literary critic. When he tells Orestes not to stay to listen to Electra, he is telling the younger poet what voices to listen to, what voices to ignore. Later, Orestes will show that he has learned this lesson of discrimination. After the recognition scene, when Electra, again in lyric meter, begins to recall the sorrows of the past, Orestes with his iambic lines cuts her off:

τὰ μὲν περισσεύοντα τῶν λόγων ἄφες,
καὶ μήτε μήτηρ ὡς κακὴ δίδασκέ με
μήθ' ὡς πατρῴαν κτῆσιν Αἴγισθος δόμων
ἀντλεῖ, τὰ δ' ἐκχεῖ, τὰ δὲ διασπείρει μάτην·

Electra 1288-91

Give up excess of words,
and don't teach me that our mother is evil
nor that Aegisthus uses up the paternal property of our home
and squanders it, and scatters it uselessly.[63]

The Paidagogos at the end of this early scene not only tells Orestes what to avoid listening to, namely, the lyric lines of Electra, but also tells him what he should heed and act upon— the commands of Apollo, the ultimate poetic authority (82-83). There is a hierarchy, and in it nothing comes before the orders of Apollo (μηδὲν πρόσθεν ἢ τὰ Λοξίου 82). With the hortatory subjunctive πειρώμεθα 'let us attempt', the Paidagogos is the leader who directs and inspires and leads Orestes to follow the poetic voice that has the greatest power and authority, the voice of Apollo.

The Paidagogos' last lines before the three men leave the stage reflect the importance of the issues of authority, speech, action, and drama. The Paidagogos insists that Orestes act (ἔρδειν 83) on the orders of the ultimate authority, Apollo. He urges Orestes with the verb ἀρχηγετεῖν, sometimes translated 'to make a fair beginning'.[64] But as has been observed, "ἀρχηγετεῖν means to start off in a disciplined way from some central authority. The word had special Spartan associations (their

---

[63] For the male domination of female lamentation, see Loraux 1986.44-50, where, in the context of a discussion of the **thrênos** 'lament', she cites the case of Theseus and Adrastus in Euripides' *Suppliant Women*. In this play, Theseus, faced with the overwhelming lamentation of women, invites Adrastus to speak in order to put an end to the women's mourning. As Loraux puts it, "To deliver [**meligêrus Adrastos** 'Adrastus of the honeyed words'] from the epic and to direct him to his vocation as orator, Theseus has to pull him out of the female world of the lament...." There is a clear parallel between Theseus and the Paidagogos, who keeps Orestes away from Electra's lament. Theseus and Orestes, too, are similar—they both control and manipulate the speech of those around them. On the traditions of women's laments as appropriated by tragedy, see also, in general, Loraux 1990 .

[64] Jebb 1894 translation of line 83.

kings were called ἀρχαγέται)."[65] In effect, the Paidagogos is telling Orestes to act as king, to assume the role of leader. He then immediately reminds Orestes of the rightful king, Agamemnon, and Orestes' duty and obligation to him, by instructing him to pour forth the libations for his father (84).

Using the verb φημί 'I declare' (85), [66] the Paidagogos ends his last lines with an emphasis on his own speech. He 'declares' that these actions bring victory and κράτος [kratos] 'power'. But it is a special kind of power, κράτος τῶν δρωμένων 'kratos over the things being done [drômenôn from the verb draô]'. As noted, the verb draô is related to the noun drama 'drama, the things done on stage'.[67] Spoken here by the Paidagogos, the poet/actor who is about to deliver the messenger speech to Clytemnestra, this phrase can mean 'power over the the things of the drama'. For the Paidagogos knows that those who control both the poetry of the theater and its illusions will have victory, νίκη, over Clytemnestra and Aegisthus.

With the words κράτος τῶν δρωμένων 'power over the things of the drama', the three men exit, having given the audience the opportunity to see Orestes' nature and that of the Paidagogos and the relationship between the two men. Orestes is a figure like Odysseus, a poet/king who will establish his authority through his poetic voice. The Paidagogos, Orestes' teacher, is the older poet to whom Orestes looks for inspiration and guidance. We see Orestes in the process of developing his own poetic voice, that of the dramatic poet. In this first scene of the play he instructs the Paidagogos on the speech that he is to give to Clytemnestra. In a later scene (680-763), Orestes will

[65] Kells 1973 at lines 82ff of the *Electra*.

[66] The conjecture preferred by Pearson 1924, Kells 1973, Kamerbeek 1974, Dawe 1984, and Lloyd-Jones and Wilson 1990a. For discussion, see Lloyd-Jones and Wilson 1990b.44.

[67] For the connection between the verb draô/dran and drama, see pp. 16-17 above.

indeed successfully incorporate the voice of the epic poet, the older man, into the poetry of the theater.

Orestes will assume control over the poetic tradition, thus enabling himself to assume control over Mycenae. As we shall see, many voices are now competing for authority in Mycenae; there are many versions of stories and justifications for actions. Orestes is entering into a contest of words. His poetry, the poetry of drama, will eventually triumph over all others, for with his relationship to the Paidagogos, the older poet, and with his relationship to Agamemnon, the rightful ruler of Mycenae, his words have the **sophia** of the poet and the authority of the king. Orestes is a man of words and a man of actions, the man whose words will be actions—the performance of the play.

CHAPTER 2

Different Voices, Different Stories

We now consider the words and stories that the women in Mycenae have tried to establish as true. Electra, like Orestes, and like Clytemnestra, is a poet figure. In her exchange with Clytemnestra (516-659), she is the traditional poet who uses praise and blame to try to establish **dikê** 'justice'.[1] She has been in a poetic contest with Clytemnestra, a contest in which each woman takes the stance of the praise/blame poet who speaks for the community. Each woman has a different version of the past: Clytemnestra tells the story that defends her actions;

---

[1] For the social function of poetry as blame or praise, see Dumézil 1969 and Detienne 1973.18-27. For expressions of blame and their social function in the context of epic poetry, see Vodoklys 1992.

Electra, the story that condemns them.[2] We shall see that
without the traditional male authority figure—here, Aegisthus
or Orestes—to give their stories power, neither can overcome
the other; they are caught in an unending contest of words.[3]

As we have seen, Electra's first words in the play can
momentarily move her audience, but not change their actions.[4]
The emotional impact of her first lyric line, ἰώ μοί μοι δύστηνος
'Alas for me, wretched one' (77), is enough to delay the exit of
Orestes and his two companions. But the Paidagogos' reply to
Orestes' question of whether they should stay to listen to
Electra is the abrupt ἥκιστα 'not at all' (82). Nothing is to
interfere with their actions (82-84), because these actions are
what bring **nikê** 'victory' and κράτος τῶν δρωμένων 'power over
the things being done' (85). Electra's performance must be
dismissed because her lyrical lament, though beautiful, is
powerless.[5] Hers is traditional lyric poetry, poetry without the
actions of the drama. Only drama, which includes actions and
words, which makes words actions, will have power in
Mycenae.

When Electra enters (86), she loses her potential male
audience. Their departure and the rest of her first speech reveal
her constant isolation and the inability of her poetry to change

---

[2] For a discussion of the nature and function of different versions of stories
told by different characters in Sophocles, see Roberts 1989, respect for which
is reflected in the above chapter title.

[3] For the argument between Clytemnestra and Electra as one that is long-
standing and "without hope of resolution," see Blundell 1989.161-72. For an
interesting alternative view, see Kitzinger 1991.311-17, where she also sees
this scene as a verbal **agôn** 'contest', but with Electra the victor on the moral
grounds of justice.

[4] See pp. 41-44 above.

[5] For an appreciation of the beauty of the kommos and parodos, see the
commentaries of Jebb 1894 and Kells 1973 and the analysis of Burton
1980.188-94.

the actions of others. She is without a human audience, with only the sun and air to address:

ὦ φάος ἁγνὸν
καὶ γῆς ἰσόμοιρ᾽ ἀήρ, ὥς μοι
πολλὰς μὲν θρήνων ᾠδάς,
πολλὰς δ᾽ ἀντήρεις ᾔσθου
στέρνων πλαγὰς αἱμασσομένων,
ὁπόταν δνοφερὰ νὺξ ὑπολειφθῇ·

Electra 86-91

O pure light
and air sharing earth equally with light, how
many [**pollas**] strains of threnodies [**thrênoi**], how
many [**pollas**] opposing
blows [**plagai**] of the bleeding breast you have heard,
whenever dark night ends.

Not only does Electra reveal her isolation here, but with the repetition of **pollas** 'many' emphatically placed at the beginning of succeeding lines (88-89), Electra makes clear that this is not the first time that she has sung her grief in vain. By her phrasing, she also suggests that the music of her lament has many times met opposing words. The word **pollas** first modifies 'strains' (88) and then is repeated to modify 'opposing blows' (89-90). But the placing of the words first suggests that Electra is saying, 'How many strains of threnodies, and how many opposing strains you have heard'. This effect results from **pollas** first appearing in a μέν 'on the one hand' clause where it modifies ᾠδάς 'strains'. The repetition of **pollas** then occurs in the balancing δέ 'on the other hand' clause in the next line, and is so placed that at first the contrast seems to be between 'many strains' in the first clause, and 'many opposing strains', with 'strains' understood, in the contrasting clause:

πολλὰς μὲν θρήνων ᾠδάς,
πολλὰς δ᾽ ἀντήρεις ᾔσθου

[how] many strains of threnodies,
and how many opposing strains you have heard

Electra's first lines then suggest that her words have been opposed by those of others in a poetic contest.[6] In her next lines we find a further suggestion of this opposition:

τὰ δὲ παννυχίδων κήδη στυγεραὶ
ξυνίσασ᾿ εὐναὶ μογερῶν οἴκων,

Electra 92-93

The cares of my nightly festivals—the hateful
bed of my wretched home knows them well....

Electra says that her bed knows the cares of the παννυχίδες, sometimes translated 'vigils'; but, as has been pointed out, the word παννυχίς is properly a 'joyous torch-festival', such as the one held at the Lenaea (Aristophanes *Frogs* 371) and at the Bendideia (Plato *Republic* 328a).[7] We shall see that, when Electra refers to her own laments as 'festivals', she is making a comparison between her own poetry and that of Clytemnestra. As noted, Electra will soon say that her mother has also established a festival.[8] Having determined the day of Agamemnon's death, Clytemnestra 'establishes a **khoros**' (280) in order to celebrate the event with music and dance. With her reference to 'festivals', Electra is speaking ironically of her own opposing 'celebration' in which she tells her version of her father's death. His death is not a cause for a festival such as

---

[6] This opposition will be evident in her exchange with Clytemnestra (516-659), discussed below.

[7] For this definition of παννυχίδες and these references, see Jebb 1894 at lines 92f of the *Electra*. For other discussions of παννυχίδες as festivals, see Kells 1973 at lines 86ff and Lloyd-Jones and Wilson 1990b at lines 92-93 of the *Electra*.

[8] For a discussion of this passage, see pp. 31-32 above.

the **khoros** that her mother produces, but is the occasion for lament:

ὅσα τὸν δύστηνον ἐμὸν <u>θρηνῶ</u>
πατέρ᾽, ὃν κατὰ μὲν βάρβαρον αἶαν
φοίνιος Ἄρης οὐκ ἐξένισεν,
μήτηρ δ᾽ ἡμὴ χὠ κοινολεχὴς
Αἴγισθος, ὅπως δρῦν ὑλοτόμοι,
σχίζουσι κάρα φονίῳ πελέκει·

Electra 94-99

how often <u>I lament with the threnody</u> [**thrêneô**] my unfortunate
father, whom bloody Ares did not keep
as guest in a foreign land,
but rather, my mother and the sharer of her bed
Aegisthus, as woodsmen do to oak,
split his head with a murderous axe.

As Electra tells us about her laments for her father, she refers to the actual form of her song with the noun **thrênoi** 'threnodies' (88) and then uses the related verb **thrêneô** 'lament with the threnody' (94). She is an artist telling the audience about her art, as she speaks of her **thrênoi** while actually singing one. Like Sophocles' play the *Electra*, the opening lines of the character Electra are a work of art about a work of art, a threnody about threnodies.

Electra concludes the tale of her father's death with a commentary on her story's effect:

κοὐδεὶς τούτων οἶκτος ἀπ᾽ ἄλλης
ἢ ᾽μοῦ φέρεται, σοῦ, πάτερ, οὕτως
αἰκῶς οἰκτρῶς τε θανόντος.

Electra 100-102

And for these things no pity is born
from any other but me, for you, father, so
cruelly and piteously killed.

At the very moment that the audience hear the beauty of
Electra's poetry, they hear Electra tell of its ineffectiveness: her
lament for her father inspires pity in no one (100-101). The
audience of the *Electra* feel the beauty of her song, while hearing
of its powerlessness.

As Electra continues, she again refers to her own **thrênoi**,

ἀλλ᾽ οὐ μὲν δὴ
λήξω θρήνων στυγερῶν τε γόων,

Electra 103-4

But I will not
cease from my threnodies [**thrênoi**] and hateful weeping,

and compares herself to another mournful singer, saying that
she will cry aloud to all, 'like some nightingale having lost its
young' (τεκνολέτειρ᾽ ὥς τις ἀηδών 107).[9]

In the **thrênos** Electra pictures herself as the poet, the
nightingale, who sings her version of her father's death (91-109)
and laments the failure of her lament to inspire pity in others
(100-102).[10] But at the end of Electra's **thrênos**, we find that
she does have one audience sympathetic to her tale. The chorus
of Mycenaean women enter, and their first words show that,
though critical of the constancy of her lament, they are
sympathetic to her cause:

ὦ παῖ, παῖ δυστανοτάτας
Ἠλέκτρα ματρός, τίν᾽ ἀεὶ
λάσκεις ὧδ᾽ ἀκόρεστον οἰμωγὰν
τὸν πάλαι ἐκ δολερᾶς ἀθεώτατα
ματρὸς ἁλόντ᾽ ἀπάταις Ἀγαμέμνονα

---

[9] For Electra and the image of the nightingale, see Loraux 1990.92-95.
[10] For the nightingale as poet, see Hesiod *Works and Days* 202-12 and
discussion in Nagy 1990a.65-66.

κακᾷ τε χειρὶ πρόδοτον; ὣς ὁ τάδε πορὼν
ὄλοιτ', εἴ μοι θέμις τάδ' αὐδᾶν.

Electra 121-27

Child, child of a most wretched
mother, Electra, what is this
insatiable lamentation
that you always cry[11] in this way,
lamenting Agamemnon, caught long ago most wickedly
by the deceptions of your treacherous mother
and betrayed by an evil hand? So may the one who did these things
perish, if it is permitted for me to say these things.

The chorus believe Electra's version of the story of
Agamemnon's death, seeing it as an evil deed (124-26). With
their wish that the doer of the deed perish (126-27), they make
clear that they share in Electra's desire for the punishment of
her father's murderers. The chorus represent a portion of the
community of Mycenae who are sympathetic to Electra. They
are the **philai** 'the near and dear' with whom the poet Electra
can communicate.[12] The chorus show their sympathy not only in
what they say, but in how they say it: they respond to Electra's
opening lyric **thrênos** with lyric lines of their own and thus
enter into a **kommos** 'lyric lament', a dialogue in song with
Electra.[13]

As the exchange between the chorus and herself begins,
Electra's first words recognize the bonds of **philotês**
'friendship' that join her and the Mycenaean women:

---

[11] Note that this verb, λάσκεις, the reading preferred by Lloyd-Jones and
Wilson 1990b, is the same verb used of the cries of the nightingale in Hesiod's
Works and Days (207) as she is carried away by the falcon.

[12] For the ideal poetic audience characterized as **philos, agathos,** and
sophos, see discussion pp. 22-23 above.

[13] For the classification of the terms **thrênos** and **kommos,** see Alexiou
1974.102-3.

ἀλλ', ὦ παντοίας φιλότητος ἀμειβόμεναι χάριν...

Electra 134

But, you, exchanging [with me] the joy of friendship in every form....

Electra is like the poet, and the chorus of Mycenaean women are her community. This **kommos** (121-250) combined with the **thrênos** that Electra has already sung (77-120) form the longest lyric passage that we find in Sophocles. In this long, lyric showpiece, Electra is like a χορηγός 'chorus leader', such as Hagesikhora in Alcman (PMG 1.44), the soloist who takes the lead in a large choral production. Electra's opening lyric solo and her exchange with the chorus in the **kommos** form a choral work within the drama. Sophocles, through Electra, makes the audience of his play feel the power and beauty of choral poetry. Then he immediately makes his audience realize that even its sheer beauty and power to move the audience is not enough to change things in Mycenae. As Electra says after the **kommos** ends, she still sees the πήματα 'woes' (258) of her father's house:

ἀγὼ κατ' ἦμαρ καὶ κατ' εὐφρόνην ἀεὶ
θάλλοντα μᾶλλον ἢ καταφθίνονθ' ὁρῶ

Electra 259-60

[woes] which by day and by night I see
always flourishing rather than perishing....

Electra describes the outrages in her father's house, the outrages that her laments do not change. She stresses first the visual, 'seeing' (ὁρῶσα) the woes of her father's house (258). As she continues, she describes these troubles as those that she 'sees' (ὁρῶ) flourishing (260). She is indignant whenever she 'sees' (ἴδω) Aegisthus sitting on her father's throne (267-68), whenever she 'sees' (εἰσίδω) him wearing her father's robes (268-69), whenever she 'sees' (ἴδω) him in her father's bed (271-73).

Electra, who has used a medium of sound, the music and words of the **thrênos** and **kommos**, now insists on the power of the visual. It is the sight of Aegisthus that so angers her. Soon she will speak of the sounds—the words of Clytemnestra's blame poetry—that affect her. But first she repeats that it is the things she sees that afflict her. Electra has control only of sound; Aegisthus and Clytemnestra have, as we see here, control over the visual. It is the picture of Aegisthus impersonating, as it were, her father that overcomes her, as he sits on the throne, wears Agamemnon's robes, and lies in Agamemnon's bed (267-73). This insistence on the power of the visual and the fact that Aegisthus and Clytemnestra control this power, prepare the audience for what will be the ultimate struggle in Mycenae. It will be a struggle that involves not simply control of language, but control of appearances. The Paidagogos and Orestes are about to enter into a dramatic contest with Aegisthus and Clytemnestra, a contest in which the victors will be those who best control not only the poetry, but also the spectacle of the drama (**theatron**).

Having spoken of the effect of the sight of Aegisthus on her, Electra speaks of the effect of what she hears. She imagines the sound of Clytemnestra laughing as she establishes her **khoros**:

ἀλλ᾽ ὥσπερ ἐγγελῶσα τοῖς ποιουμένοις,
εὑροῦσ᾽ ἐκείνην ἡμέραν, ἐν ᾗ τότε
πατέρα τὸν ἀμὸν ἐκ δόλου κατέκτανεν,
ταύτῃ χοροὺς ἵστησι

Electra 277-80

But, as though laughing at things done,
having found the day on which she
killed my father by treachery,
on that day she establishes a chorus [**khorous histêsi**]....

Electra describes the effect on herself of the sound of her mother's laughter and the music of the **khoros** with which she celebrates Agamemnon's death: Electra mourns, but usually not in public. She sees herself as an inarticulate mourner, who cries, not in front of others, but within the house and alone. When she sees her mother's **khoros** and sacrificial offerings of thanks for 'deliverance' (280-81), Electra says of herself,

ἐγὼ δ᾽ ὁρῶσα δύσμορος κατὰ στέγας
κλαίω, τέτηκα, κἀπικωκύω πατρὸς
τὴν δυστάλαιναν δαῖτ᾽ ἐπωνομασμένην
αὐτὴ πρὸς αὐτήν·

Electra 282-85

I, ill-fated, when I see [these things] in the house
weep, waste away and lament over the
wretched feast, named in my father's honor,
[I weep] myself to myself.

In her description of Clytemnestra and herself, Electra indicates that there is no audience for her laments; she is in the house (282) and weeps to herself alone, αὐτὴ πρὸς αὐτήν (285). Electra's are the inarticulate sounds of the weeping mourner (283). In contrast, as Electra describes her, Clytemnestra's sounds are articulated in words. She has established the **khoros**, a very sophisticated, public form of words and music.

Describing Clytemnestra's response to her laments, Electra says that she cannot weep to the full measure of her desire (285-6) because Clytemnestra, taking the stance of a blame poet, reproaches her:

αὕτη γὰρ ἡ λόγοισι γενναία γυνὴ
φωνοῦσα τοιάδ᾽ ἐξονειδίζει κακά,

Electra 287-88

For this woman, noble in words,
saying these harsh things reproaches [**exoneidizei**]....

With the word **exoneidizei** 'reproaches' Electra indicates that Clytemnestra uses the language of the blame poet. Then Electra quotes Clytemnestra directly:

"ὦ δύσθεον μίσημα, σοὶ μόνῃ πατὴρ
τέθνηκεν; ἄλλος δ᾽ οὔτις ἐν πένθει βροτῶν;
κακῶς ὄλοιο...."

Electra 289-91

"O impious and hateful, for you alone has a father
died? Is no one else of mortals in a state of grief?
May you perish in an evil way...."

By directly quoting Clytemnestra, Electra stresses the importance of the actual words her mother speaks. Electra herself is acting as a poet of blame when she repeats Clytemnestra's words. With her reproach of Clytemnestra's reproach, Electra follows a poetic tradition found in the *Odyssey*.[14] When Odysseus speaks to them, the disloyal handmaidens laugh at him and Melantho reproaches him (*Odyssey* 18.320-36). By ridiculing and rebuking Odysseus, these women are taking the stance of unrighteous blame poets.[15] Odysseus, in turn, speaks of Melantho as a κύων 'dog' (*Odyssey* 18.338), a term of reproach for the unrighteous blame poet.[16] Later, Eurykleia speaks of the handmaidens, calling them κύνες 'dogs' and referring to their speech as a λώβη 'disgrace' and as αἴσχεα 'acts of baseness' (19.372-4). Eurykleia is reproaching the handmaidens for their ridicule of Odysseus and is making the handmaidens' words of blame the cause of her own blame

---

[14] For this example and discussion of it in terms of blame and counterblame, see Nagy 1979.256-57.

[15] For more on the significance and function of the maids of Odysseus and their laughter, see Levine 1987.

[16] For κύων and its derivatives as traditional words of insult in blame poetry, see Faust 1970 and 1969.109-25 and Nagy 1979.226-27.

of them. Similarly, Electra makes Clytemnestra's very words of blame a cause for censure.

As Electra describes it, Clytemnestra, in the context of her own festival, the **khoros** that she produces, is the articulate blame poet. Surrounded by her own supporters, she is in command of language, both in the **khoros** and in the language of blame. Electra is reduced to being the inarticulate mourner, alone, without an audience. At this moment on stage, however, with Clytemnestra absent, Electra is surrounded by her own **philai**, the sympathetic, though powerless, women of Mycenae, and under these conditions she attempts to be a blame poet. Like Eurykleia, she sees words of reproach, in this case the words of Clytemnestra, as a cause for her own words of blame. She sees Clytemnestra's words as an outrage, closing her quotation of Clytemnestra with τάδ' ἐξυβρίζει 'these things she says insolently' (293).

By quoting her, Electra both blames Clytemnestra and shows the queen at her most powerful. But then Electra reveals that there is one speech that controls Clytemnestra. She continues:

τάδ' ἐξυβρίζει· πλὴν ὅταν κλύῃ τινὸς
ἥξοντ' Ὀρέστην· τηνικαῦτα δ' ἐμμανὴς
βοᾷ παραστᾶσ', "οὐ σύ μοι τῶνδ' αἰτία;"

Electra 293-95

These things she says insolently; except when she hears from someone
that Orestes is about to come; then, raving,
she comes up to me and shouts, "Don't I have you to blame for all this?"

A mere story, the report that Orestes has come, has a violent effect on Clytemnestra. Just as at the end of the prologue Orestes was affected by the sound of Electra's voice (77-81),[17]

---

[17] See pp. 41-43 above.

so here Clytemnestra is affected by the sound of someone telling her that Orestes is in Mycenae. She becomes more frantic in her reproach of Electra. She now 'raves' (ἐμμανής) and 'shouts' (βοᾷ) (294-95). She blames Electra for what should be a cause of joy, not blame—the return of Orestes (295). Again, to quote directly Clytemnestra's words of unjustified blame is a way for the blame poet, Electra, in turn, to reproach Clytemnestra.

Electra marks the end of her quotation of Clytemnestra with the phrase τοιαῦθ᾽ ὑλακτεῖ 'such things she barks' (299). Like Odysseus and Eurykleia when they speak of the handmaidens as 'dogs', Electra pictures Clytemnestra as a dog that 'barks out' its insults. With this image of the dog, Electra characterizes Clytemnestra in the traditional terms of the unrighteous blame poet.

Electra concludes with her own words of blame as she ridicules both Clytemnestra and Aegisthus:

> σὺν δ᾽ ἐποτρύνει πέλας
> ὁ κλεινὸς αὐτῇ ταὐτὰ νυμφίος παρών,
> ὁ πάντ᾽ ἄναλκις οὗτος, ἡ πᾶσα βλάβη,
> ὁ σὺν γυναιξὶ τὰς μάχας ποιούμενος.

Electra 299-302

> right at her side
> her renowned bridegroom urges the same things,
> that completely impotent man, a total disaster,
> a man who does his fighting with women.

With her ridicule of Aegisthus, Electra appears to be as able a blame poet as Clytemnestra. However, as Electra has pointed out, Clytemnestra and Aegisthus, in addition to having the power of words, also have the power of the visual, and thus have the combined forces of the drama. They present the visual image of their control of the kingship in the form of Aegisthus playing the role of Agamemnon—sitting on Agamemnon's throne, wearing his clothes, sleeping in his wife's bed (266-74).

Clytemnestra has also set up her own drama, a **khoros** in celebration of Agamemnon's death. Electra, with only the power of poetry, is helpless before their combined powers of the theater. It will take another playwright and another production, that of Orestes, to overcome the dramatic display of Clytemnestra and Aegisthus.

In her next exchange with the chorus, Electra portrays Aegisthus as the man who, like the playwright, controls characters' speech and entrances on stage. First, we see the power of Aegisthus, merely by his presence, to control the speech of Electra and the chorus. The women are anxious to know whether Aegisthus is close by:

φέρ᾽ εἰπέ, πότερον ὄντος Αἰγίσθου πέλας
λέγεις τάδ᾽ ἡμῖν, ἢ βεβῶτος ἐκ δόμων;

Electra 310-11

Come, tell us, is Aegisthus near
when you say these things, or gone from home?

Electra assures them that he is absent:

ἦ κάρτα· μὴ δόκει μ᾽ ἄν, εἴπερ ἦν πέλας,
θυραῖον οἰχνεῖν· νῦν δ᾽ ἀγροῖσι τυγχάνει.

Electra 312-13

Certainly. Don't think that, if he were near,
I would come outside; he is in the country now.

Electra repeats the chorus' word πέλας 'near' in the same place in which they used it, at the end of the first line in the exchange, thus emphasizing the importance of Aegisthus' proximity. If he were near, she would not be outside. Despite her remarks, the chorus is still cautious about speaking (314-15), and Electra must again assure them that he is gone and they may speak (316). If Aegisthus were present, he would, in effect, prevent Electra from making her entrance to her audience, the sympathetic Mycenaean women, and there would have been no public speech, no performance of poetry in the **kommos** 'lyric exchange' between Electra and her community. We see that Aegisthus, when he is present, controls entrances and speech.

The chorus now wish to know about Electra's brother and Electra responds:

> Χο. καὶ δή σ' ἐρωτῶ, τοῦ κασιγνήτου τί φής,
> ἥξοντος, ἢ μέλλοντος; εἰδέναι θέλω.
> Ηλ. φησίν γε· φάσκων δ'οὐδὲν ὧν λέγει ποεῖ.

Electra 317-19

> Ch. And I ask you, what do you have to say about your brother,
> is he about to come, or delaying? I want to know.
> El. He says he is; he talks, but does nothing of what he says.

Now the exchange between Electra and the chorus, which has just brought out Aegisthus' control of actions and words, brings up the question of Orestes' words and actions. In Electra's response to the chorus there are three words of speaking, φησίν, φάσκων, λέγει, followed by the single word of action ποεῖ 'he does' which is in an emphatic position at the end of the line (319). Electra raises the possibility that there will be more speech than action. If Orestes only talks about coming and never does it, he will be like Electra, who has the ability to speak, in the form of the **thrênos** or in the language of the blame poet, but not the power to act.

The exchange between Electra and the chorus ends when the chorus warn Electra not to speak further:

> μὴ νῦν ἔτ' εἴπῃς μηδέν· ὡς δόμων ὁρῶ
> τὴν σὴν ὅμαιμον...

Electra 324-25

> Don't say anything more now; for I see
> your sister coming from the house ....

Again the entrance of someone else controls speech. Just as at the end of the prologue Electra's entrance affected the actions of Orestes and the Paidagogos by delaying their exit, so the entrance of Chrysothemis affects the speech of Electra and the chorus. Chrysothemis is on better terms with Clytemnestra and Aegisthus than is her sister. The effect of her entrance, which silences the speech of the chorus and Electra, suggests that Aegisthus' control can be felt even through a powerless character, if that character is in some way connected to him.

The exchange between Chrysothemis and Electra concerns the relative merits of speech and silence. It also concerns the idea of teaching in the repeated use of the verb **didaskô** 'to teach', the verb used of the poet when he produces and directs a play.[18] In the first half of their exchange, Electra and Chrysothemis argue, using the language of blame, as each claims the right to 'teach' (**didaskô**) the other. But by the second half of the scene, Chrysothemis, moved by Electra's words and those of the chorus, changes her position.

The importance of words is stressed in Chrysothemis' opening lines. The first thing that she wants to know is what Electra has been saying:

τίν' αὖ σὺ τήνδε πρὸς θυρῶνος ἐξόδοις
ἐλθοῦσα φωνεῖς, ὦ κασιγνήτη, φάτιν

Electra 328-29

What [tina] speech [phatin] have you come out of doors again
to utter, my sister?

The placement of **tina** 'what' and the word it modifies **phatin** 'speech' is significant: each word occurs in a prominent position—**tina** at the beginning of the line and **phatin** at the

---

[18] See, for example, Taplin 1977.12-15 and Blundell 1989.12-16 for discussion and bibliography on the poet as teacher.

end. But, to increase further the focus on **phatin** 'speech', it comes, not at the end of the same line as that of **tina**, but a whole line later, with the sound 'tin' in both words punctuating the beginning and end of the extraordinary two line separation. That these two lines are Chrysothemis' first in the play stresses the importance to her of Electra's words.

In addition to wanting to know exactly what Electra says (What speech?), Chrysothemis is also concerned about where Electra says it (328-29). Electra has come 'out of doors', and it is what Electra says before her fellow Mycenaeans, her audience, that concerns her sister.

Independently of Electra and the chorus, Chrysothemis then reintroduces the issue of the vanity of words without action:

κοὐδ᾽ ἐν χρόνῳ μακρῷ διδαχθῆναι θέλεις
θυμῷ ματαίῳ μὴ χαρίζεσθαι κενά;

Electra 330-31

Don't you want to be taught in the long course of time
not to indulge in vain your useless anger?

Just as Electra criticized Orestes for talking about coming but never acting on his words (319), so Chrysothemis points out the ineffectiveness of Electra's coming outside to speak when what she does cannot affect Aegisthus and Clytemnestra.

Chrysothemis also wonders that Electra is not willing 'to be taught' (she uses a form of **didaskô**) that her speech in public is in vain. Chrysothemis thus suggests that someone is doing this 'teaching'. As we have just seen (310-16), Electra would not be outside and the chorus would not be willing to speak if Aegisthus were present. There is the suggestion here, made explicit later by Clytemnestra (516-20), that Aegisthus is the one who usually 'teaches' or 'directs' Electra's action and speech and can force her to be silent.

Chrysothemis is the advocate of silence. She continues, saying that she would show how she feels, if only she had strength:

καίτοι τοσοῦτόν γ'οἶδα κἀμαυτήν, ὅτι
ἀλγῶ 'πὶ τοῖς παροῦσιν· ὥστ' ἄν, εἰ σθένος
λάβοιμι, δηλώσαιμ' ἂν οἷ' αὐτοῖς φρονῶ.
νῦν δ' ἐν κακοῖς μοι πλεῖν ὑφειμένῃ δοκεῖ,
καὶ μὴ δοκεῖν μὲν δρᾶν τι, πημαίνειν δὲ μή.
τοιαῦτα δ' ἄλλα καὶ σὲ βούλομαι ποεῖν.

Electra 332-37

And yet to this extent at least I know myself, that
I am grieved at the present circumstances; so that, if I could find strength,
I would show them what sort of thoughts I have toward them.
But now I think it's best for me to sail in these troubles with sails
trimmed, and not to seem to do something, but cause them no distress.
Such things I wish you to do also.

Chrysothemis reproaches Electra for the same reason that Electra reproached Orestes (319): the vanity of words without action. Knowing that she is powerless to hurt Aegisthus and Clytemnestra, Chrysothemis does not show them how she feels. Unlike Electra, she is unwilling to come forth and speak.

Though conceding that justice is on Electra's side (338-39), Chrysothemis still ends her first speech by advocating compliance:

εἰ δ' ἐλευθέραν με δεῖ
ζῆν, τῶν κρατούντων ἐστὶ πάντ' ἀκουστέα.

Electra 339-40

If I am to live as a free woman,
all orders of the rulers must be obeyed [akoustea].

Significantly, Chrysothemis' word for 'obeying' is a word whose fundamental sense is that of hearing, **akoustea**. To comply is to 'listen' to those in power. Chrysothemis' first speech in the play began with a critical questioning of Electra's words, 'What...speech?' (τίνα...φάτιν 328-9), and ends with **akoustea**, advocating silence in the form of listening and obeying.

Electra finds it strange that Chrysothemis has forgotten her father and is so concerned about her mother (341-42). She identifies what, in her opinion, is the source of Chrysothemis' reproach and her argument for silence and obedience:

ἅπαντα γάρ σοι τἀμὰ νουθετήματα
κείνης διδακτά, κοὐδὲν ἐκ σαυτῆς λέγεις.

Electra 343-44

For all the reproaches you have for me
are the teachings of that woman, and nothing you say is your own.

In effect, Electra sees Clytemnestra as the playwright who directs her player to use the language of blame, νουθετήματα 'reproaches'. Just as Orestes uses the Paidagogos and instructs him to use the language of epic in his speech to Clytemnestra, so Electra sees Clytemnestra as the playwright who composes a part for her player, Chrysothemis. All of Chrysothemis' reproaches, her first lines of the play, are not her own words, κοὐδὲν ἐκ σαυτῆς λέγεις 'nothing you say is your own', but are the lines taught by Clytemnestra, κείνης διδακτά 'taught by that woman'.

Further on in her speech, Electra challenges Chrysothemis' argument for silence, again using the verb **didaskô**:

ἐπεὶ δίδαξον, ἢ μάθ᾽ ἐξ ἐμοῦ, τί μοι
κέρδος γένοιτ᾽ ἂν τῶνδε ληξάσῃ γόων.

Electra 352-53

For explain [**didaxon**], or learn from me, what
profit there would be for me if I cease from my laments.

Later, Clytemnestra will use the same word, **didaxon**, the imperative form of **didaskô**, in the same way, when she challenges Electra to 'explain' Agamemnon's sacrifice of Iphigenia (534). In this exchange between the two sisters, where Chrysothemis is represented as the mouthpiece of Clytemnestra, there are indications of what the issues are between Electra and her mother. This scene is a preview to the one between Clytemnestra and Electra that follows (517-59). Each woman tries to be the director who 'instructs' (**didaskô**) the other players, and each tries to be the righteous blame poet, who finds the reproach of the other a thing blameworthy in itself.

Electra continues to insist on the rightness of her position, while reproaching Chrysothemis for her relationship with Clytemnestra and Aegisthus (354-68). Finally, the chorus begs each side to listen to the other (369-71), and in response Chrysothemis tells them why she has brought up the subject of Electra's behavior toward her mother and Aegisthus: she has heard that Electra is threatened with a κακὸν μέγιστον 'a very great evil' (374).

Electra's response is in the form of a contest of words:

φέρ᾽ εἰπὲ δὴ τὸ δεινόν. εἰ γὰρ τῶνδέ μοι
μεῖζόν τι λέξεις, οὐκ ἂν ἀντείποιμ᾽ ἔτι.

Electra 376-77

Come, say the terrible thing. For if you tell me something
greater than these, I would not speak in opposition anymore.

In two lines Electra uses three verbs of speaking, εἰπέ 'say', λέξεις 'tell', ἀντείποιμι 'speak in opposition', challenging Chrysothemis to try to overcome her in a match of words.

Chrysothemis recognizes that this is a verbal contest with the opening of her rebuttal, ἀλλ᾽ ἐξερῶ σοι 'but I will tell you' (378) and then begins to describe the 'very great evil'. It is a threat from Clytemnestra and Aegisthus, and Chrysothemis puts it in terms of sound and light. They will punish Electra for speech, for voicing her laments, and the punishment will be imprisonment in a lightless chamber. Chrysothemis pictures Electra there singing:

μέλλουσι γάρ σ᾽, εἰ τῶνδε μὴ λήξεις γόων,
ἐνταῦθα πέμψειν ἔνθα μήποθ᾽ ἡλίου
φέγγος προσόψῃ, ζῶσα δ᾽ ἐν κατηρεφεῖ
στέγῃ χθονὸς τῆσδ᾽ ἐκτὸς ὑμνήσεις κακά.

Electra 379-81

For they intend, if you do not cease from these laments,
to send you there where you will never see the sun's
light, and, living in a covered
chamber, far from this land, you will sing your sorrows.

Chrysothemis envisions Electra deprived of light (380-81) and deprived of audience, 'far from this land' (381). She will still sing (381), but without any possibility of being seen or heard. Electra's threatened punishment is the extreme form of the conditions under which she has already been living. Aegisthus, when present, has been able to keep Electra indoors and off stage, deprived of the stage and deprived of her audience.

Yet Electra refuses to change. To Chrysothemis' insistence that Electra be sensible (394), Electra replies that she will not be taught:

Ηλ. μή μ᾽ ἐκδίδασκε τοῖς φίλοις εἶναι κακήν.
Χρ. ἀλλ᾽ οὐ διδάσκω· τοῖς κρατοῦσι δ᾽εἰκαθεῖν.

Electra 395-96

El.   Do not teach [ek-didaskô] me to be base to the near and dear.
Chr. I am not teaching [didaskô] you that, but rather, to yield to those in power.

Electra refuses to be directed by anyone. Chrysothemis at last gives up the argument and turns to her errand:

χωρήσομαί τἄρ᾽ οἷπερ ἐστάλην ὁδοῦ.

Electra 404

I shall go where I was sent.

Chrysothemis puts her own words into actions: she counsels obedience and now she demonstrates it. She is an agent in errand as she is an agent in words: she acts on behalf of Clytemnestra.

Before Chrysothemis leaves, the two women begin to discuss a new issue, the nature of Chrysothemis' errand. Clytemnestra has sent Chrysothemis to take offerings to Agamemnon's tomb. Even as they discuss this new matter, the sisters still focus on each other's speech. When Chrysothemis identifies Clytemnestra as the source of the offerings for Agamemnon, Electra is surprised:

Ηλ.   πῶς εἶπας; ἦ τῷ δυσμενεστάτῳ βροτῶν;
Χρ.   ὃν ἔκταν᾽ αὐτή· τοῦτο γὰρ λέξαι θέλεις.

Electra 407-8

El.   What are you saying? For her greatest enemy?
Chr.   Whom she herself killed. For that's what you wish to say.

Electra questions Chrysothemis' speech, 'What are you saying?' And Chrysothemis corrects hers: when Electra refers to her father as Clytemnestra's 'greatest enemy', Chrysothemis adds a line for her, 'Whom she herself killed. That's what you wish to say'. Theirs is a conversation of questioning and correcting of each others words.

As they continue, they still refer to their own acts of speaking. When Chrysothemis reports that Clytemnestra has had a terrifying vision, she is surprised at Electra's hopeful response, wondering if there is something in the dream that gives her courage (410-12). Electra responds, speaking about speech, as does Chrysothemis:

Ηλ. εἴ μοι λέγοις τὴν ὄψιν, εἴποιμ᾽ ἂν τότε.
Χρ. ἀλλ᾽ οὐ κάτοιδα πλὴν ἐπὶ σμικρὸν φράσαι.
Ηλ. λέγ᾽ ἀλλὰ τοῦτο. πολλά τοι σμικροὶ λόγοι
     ἔσφηλαν ἤδη καὶ κατώρθωσαν βροτούς.
Χρ. λόγος τις αὐτήν ἐστιν εἰσιδεῖν....

Electra 413-17

El.   If you would <u>tell</u> [**legô**] me the vision, I could then <u>say</u> [**eipon**].
Chr. But I don't know much, except to <u>say</u> [**phrazô**] a little.
El.   But <u>tell</u> [**legô**] me this. Often small <u>words</u> [**logoi**]
      have brought men down and then set them right.
Chr. There is some <u>story</u> [**logos**] that she saw....

After hearing that a dream of Agamemnon's return to Mycenae has terrified Clytemnestra (417-27), Electra begs Chrysothemis not to take their mother's offerings to Agamemnon's tomb, but rather to take locks of their own hair and the **zôma** 'girdle' of Electra, which she describes as οὐ χλιδαῖς ἠσκημένον 'not fashioned with rich ornaments' (452).

With the **zôma** of Electra, we see the second of the five props that are used in the play. In addition to the **zôma**, Sophocles uses the offerings of Clytemnestra for Agamemnon's tomb, the urn, the **sphragis** 'signet ring' of Orestes, and the veil that covers Clytemnestra's body at the end of the play. Of these, only the **sphragis** and the **zôma** are what they seem. The urn will merely appear to hold the ashes of Orestes. Clytemnestra's offerings to Agamemnon's tomb are the insincere offerings of a frightened, but not regretful, murderer, attempting to deceive his spirit with gifts to the dead. The veil concealing Clytemnestra's body is a prop used, like the urn, to deceive Aegisthus into thinking that the body it covers is not Clytemnestra's, but Orestes'.

Like the **sphragis**, the **zôma** is something genuine. When Electra describes it as 'not fashioned with rich ornaments', the word she uses for 'fashioned' is **êskêmenon**. This word is later associated with the urn, when Electra holds it and believes she is holding the remains of Orestes (1216). Orestes corrects her:

ἀλλ᾽ οὐκ Ὀρέστου, πλὴν λόγῳ γ᾽ ἠσκημένον.

Electra 1217

But they are not the remains of Orestes, except as fashioned [êskêmenon] by word [logos].

The word **êskêmenon** is from **askeô**, the verb used for the 'working' of raw materials by a craftsman. It is used of wool-making in the *Iliad* when Helen is visited by Aphrodite, disguised as a wool-dresser who 'crafted' (ἤσκειν) beautiful things from wool (*Iliad* 3.387-88). It is the verb Odysseus uses when, in response to Penelope's test, he describes the building of their bed from a tree, saying that he 'crafted' (ἀσκήσας) the bed post (*Odyssey* 23.198).

The verb is used of turning raw materials, things in their natural state, into things of culture. It is used again in the *Iliad* in the description of the making of the shield of Achilles, when Hephaestus makes a **khoros** 'dancing floor', like the one that Daedalus made for Ariadne:

ἐν δὲ χορὸν ποίκιλλε περικλυτὸς ἀμφιγυήεις,
τῷ ἴκελον οἷόν ποτ᾽ ἐνὶ Κνωσῷ εὐρείῃ
Δαίδαλος ἤσκησεν καλλιπλοκάμῳ Ἀριάδνῃ.

Iliad 18.590-92

And the renowned smith of the strong arms made elaborate on it a dancing floor [khoros], like that which once in the wide spaces of Knossos Daedalus crafted [askeô] for Ariadne of the lovely tresses.

When Orestes says that Electra is not holding the ashes of Orestes, but a thing **êskêmenon** 'fashioned' by word, he is using a term that describes the deception that he has created. Like the **khoros** that Daedalus made, Orestes has 'crafted' a play, a deception fashioned with words.

When Electra calls the **zôma** a thing 'not fashioned [**êskêmenon**] with rich ornaments', she describes her offering in terms that apply to herself. Like her gift, Electra at this point in the play is unornamented. In contrast to Chrysothemis and Orestes, she has been straightforward in her dealings with Clytemnestra and Agamemnon. Indeed, it is to tell Electra the consequences of her honesty that Chrysothemis has come: Electra is to be punished for showing her sorrow and anger (378-82). Electra's honesty threatens to bring destruction.

Orestes, in a disguise **êskêmenon** 'crafted' by word, will succeed against Clytemnestra and Aegisthus. Electra will only have success later when, having been instructed by Orestes in playing her part (1296-99), she becomes deceptive. After the moment of recognition, Orestes tells Electra that he does not want her to look radiantly happy—she would make Clytemnestra suspicious. He wishes her to look as she had before he came. Thus, he takes what had been natural emotion and appearance, Electra's grief, and turns it into art. When Orestes uses the expression 'crafted by word', he is describing the art of the stage. Like the wool of the woolmaker or the tree that Odysseus fashions into the bed, the natural emotions and appearance of Electra are raw materials that must be fashioned by the artist into the form of the play.

Electra is the example of the artist who has control of words, but uses neither the dramatic deception of Orestes nor the more passive deception of Chrysothemis. Chrysothemis' one effective action is to put her own and her sister's offerings at the tomb, instead of Clytemnestra's, an act of defiance that finally puts her own feelings against Clytemnestra and Aegisthus into actions. Hers will be deeds without words. Hers is a deception accomplished by silence. The chorus tells Chrysothemis that if she is sensible, she will put the offerings of the two sisters at the tomb—δράσεις τάδε 'you will do [**draô**] these things' (465). And Chrysothemis replies, emphasizing the action:

δράσω· τὸ γὰρ δίκαιον οὐκ ἔχει λόγον
δυοῖν ἐρίζειν, ἀλλ᾽ ἐπισπεύδει τὸ δρᾶν.
πειρωμένη δὲ τῶνδε τῶν ἔργων ἐμοὶ
σιγὴ παρ᾽ ὑμῶν πρὸς θεῶν ἔστω, φίλαι·

Electra 466-69

I will do [**draô**] them. That which is right does not give any rationale
for two people to dispute, but urges the doing [**draô**].
But for me, as I attempt these deeds [**erga**],
by the gods, let there be [**estô**] silence [**sigê**] from you, my friends.

Chrysothemis, who had come on stage saying that she was powerless to act and who had spoken words of blame that Electra declared were from her mother (343-44), now vows to act (**draô** 466) and declares that the strife between her sister and herself, the strife between the two speakers of blame, is not just (466-67). Concerning her attempt to substitute different offerings in place of Clytemnestra's, Chrysothemis hopes for one thing from the chorus—that 'there be silence' (469).

In contrast to Chrysothemis, who simply hopes for silence, Orestes is determined to establish his **muthos** 'story'. Just as Chrysothemis ends her declaration with **sigê**...**estô** 'let there be silence', so Orestes ended his summary of the story of his death that the Paidagogos was to tell with ὧδ᾽ ὁ μῦθος ἑστάτω 'let the story [**muthos**] be established [**hestatô**] to this effect' (50).[19] With the more aggressive **hestatô**, Orestes vows to 'establish a story', the purpose of which is to deceive and thus enable him to act against Clytemnestra and Aegisthus. Chrysothemis intends to act against Clytemnestra by substituting her own and Electra's offerings for Clytemnestra's. Chrysothemis does not hope, like Orestes, to establish a story to disguise her actions,

---

[19] See pp. 31-32 above.

but to use silence to hide them. Unlike Electra, both Chrysothemis and Orestes take action, one with words and one with silence. Electra with undisguised words has accomplished nothing. Chrysothemis will have a small triumph of action in silence. It is Orestes who will use both words and action to succeed against Clytemnestra and Aegisthus.

With her plea to the chorus for silence (468-71), Chrysothemis leaves the stage. At the end of the stasimon that follows, Clytemnestra enters. Now the audience see the woman who had directed her player, Chrysothemis. Clytemnestra is the one whom Electra accused of composing Chrysothemis' lines (343-44), and who directed Chrysothemis, sending her with offerings to Agamemnon's tomb (406), just as Orestes directs his own player, the Paidagogos. Chrysothemis has introduced the issues of speech, silence, praise, and blame that Clytemnestra herself will now address.

Clytemnestra begins her first speech as Chrysothemis began hers (328-31), commenting on the fact that Electra is outdoors.[20]

> ἀνειμένη μέν, ὡς ἔοικας, αὖ στρέφῃ.
> οὐ γὰρ πάρεστ᾽ Αἴγισθος, ὅς σ᾽ ἐπεῖχ᾽ ἀεὶ
> μή τοι θυραίαν γ᾽ οὖσαν αἰσχύνειν φίλους·
>
> *Electra* 516-18

> At large, so it seems, you move about once more.
> For Aegisthus is not here, who always kept you
> from being outside to shame your near and dear.

Here Clytemnestra makes the point that it is Aegisthus who controls Electra's movements, who usually keeps her indoors and off stage. We recall that the chorus had asked Electra whether or not Aegisthus was present before they felt free to

---

[20] Jebb 1894 at line 516 of the *Electra*.

speak (310 ff.). Clytemnestra's first words confirm that Aegisthus not only controls what people say, as in the case of the chorus, but also where they say it. Aegisthus can prevent Electra from being outside where she can address an audience. Just as the Paidagogos takes charge by directing the exit of the three men at the end of the prologue (73-85), thus controlling the exit of characters, so Aegisthus, like the playwright, can control entrances.

Chrysothemis had wondered that Electra had not been 'taught' (**didaskô**) to stay inside and not go outdoors to address her fellow Mycenaeans (328-31). We now find Clytemnestra explicitly saying that Aegisthus is the man who has been controlling Electra's entrances. The Paidagogos, for very different reasons, took control and deprived Electra of her audience by making Orestes and Pylades exit; similarly, Aegisthus has been the 'director' who has prevented her from entering to address an audience. Aegisthus' absence is so important that Clytemnestra repeats the fact that he is gone and says that the absence of this authority figure allows, not simply Electra's presence in public, but an opportunity for her to speak:

νῦν δ᾽ ὡς ἄπεστ᾽ ἐκεῖνος, οὐδὲν ἐντρέπῃ
ἐμοῦ γε· καίτοι πολλὰ πρὸς πολλούς με δὴ
ἐξεῖπας ὡς θρασεῖα καὶ πέρα δίκης
ἄρχω, καθυβρίζουσα καὶ σὲ καὶ τὰ σά.

Electra 519-22

Now, since he is away, you pay no attention at all
to me; and yet, you have spoken out many times to many people
about me, how, bold and beyond what's just,
I rule, outraging you and yours.

Clytemnestra complains that because Aegisthus is away, Electra pays no attention to her (519-20). Without Aegisthus, Clytemnestra has no authority: Electra is free to say what she wishes about her mother, namely, that she is bold, ruling without law, and treating her daughter with contempt (521-22). The entire scene becomes a demonstration of the impotence of words without authority. At the beginning, Clytemnestra admits that she cannot control Electra without Aegisthus. As the scene continues, Clytemnestra gives her version of the story of Agamemnon's death; Electra gives a very different one. They struggle with each other, each attempting to establish her version of the story as true. Each uses the language of the blame poet in an attempt to discredit the other. But each woman is powerless to establish one version of the story as authoritative—the contest can only be decided by the two male authority figures, Aegisthus and Orestes.

Clytemnestra continues her opening speech, saying that the conflict between Electra and herself has its source in words. Her anger has been activated by what she has heard Electra say:

> ἐγὼ δ' ὕβριν μὲν οὐκ ἔχω, κακῶς δέ σε
> λέγω κακῶς κλύουσα πρὸς σέθεν θαμά.

> *Electra* 523-24

> I am not insolent, but I speak ill of you
> because I am often spoken ill of by you.

And she knows that Electra's reason for reproaching her is the death of Agamemnon:

> πατὴρ γάρ, οὐδὲν ἄλλο, σοὶ πρόσχημ' ἀεί,
> ὡς ἐξ ἐμοῦ τέθνηκεν.

> *Electra* 525-26

> Your father—and nothing else, that's always the pretext
> [**proskhêma**]—how he died at my hands.

With the word **proskhêma** 'pretext' Clytemnestra challenges not only the truth of what Electra says, but her sincerity in saying it. The death of Agamemnon is just a 'pretext' for

Electra's reproaches. The noun comes from the verb προέχω 'hold before' and means 'that which is held before to cover, screen, cloak'. Clytemnestra begins her argument with the suggestion that Electra's laments for her father's death are not genuine.

As she begins to tell her version of the death of Agamemnon, Clytemnestra begins with Agamemnon's character. She questions Agamemnon's reasons for sacrificing her daughter Iphigenia, bringing up possible rationalizations for the deed: to please the Argives or to spare the children of his brother Menelaos by sacrificing his own in their place (534-45). She dismisses these suggestions, insisting in a rhetorical question that Agamemnon's actions were those of a father 'heedless and bad in his judgement' (ἀβούλου καὶ κακοῦ γνώμην 546). In effect, she has brought up different versions of the story of Agamemnon and dismissed them all with her argument that, no matter what his motives, there is no justification for a father's killing his own child.

Clytemnestra claims, as Electra will presently, that she is able to speak for the dead. Like the traditional poet (e.g., Hesiod *Theogony* 31-32), she claims to reveal the past accurately. Clytemnestra answers her own question of whether Agamemnon's actions were those of a father who was 'heedless and bad in his judgement', equating herself with Iphigenia in a **men** 'on the one hand'/**de** 'on the other hand' construction:

δοκῶ μέν, εἰ καὶ σῆς δίχα γνώμης λέγω.
φαίη δ᾽ ἂν ἡ θανοῦσά γ᾽, εἰ φωνὴν λάβοι.

Electra 547-48

I on the one hand [**men**] think so, even if I speak apart from your judgement. And she on the other hand [**de**], the dead girl, would say so too, if she could have voice.

Clytemnestra claims to speak the language of the past. She says what Iphigenia, a voice of an earlier time, would say if she had the power to speak. Clytemnestra imagines Iphigenia not in terms of her appearance, but in terms of her voice (548), because it is the story that matters to her and the power to tell it. Clytemnestra believes that she has the power to recreate what the voice of the past, the voice of an eyewitness of earlier events, says about the guilt of Agamemnon.

Clytemnestra ends her argument by warning Electra not to blame others before she considers the justness of her own position, ending her whole opening speech (516-51) with the verb 'blame' (ψέγε). She is characterizing Electra as a blame poet, anticipating Electra's response to her argument.

As Clytemnestra ends her argument with a verb of speaking, 'blame', Electra immediately begins hers with another, 'ἐρεῖς 'you will say' (552). Electra has two points to make, both about speech. First she wishes to make clear that Clytemnestra has started this particular conflict of words; and, second, that she, Electra, wishes permission to speak:

> ἐρεῖς μὲν οὐχὶ νῦν γέ μ᾽ ὡς ἄρξασά τι
> λυπηρὸν εἶτα σοῦ τάδ᾽ ἐξήκουσ᾽ ὕπο·
> ἀλλ᾽ ἢν ἐφῆς μοι, τοῦ τεθνηκότος θ᾽ ὕπερ
> λέξαιμ᾽ ἂν ὀρθῶς τῆς κασιγνήτης θ᾽ ὁμοῦ.

Electra 552-55

You will not say of me now at least that I began something
painful and then heard these things from you;
but, if you permit, on behalf of the dead man
I would speak correctly, and on behalf of my sister, also.

Electra emphasizes the importance of speaking and hearing. She, too, like Clytemnestra, claims to speak for the dead, in her case, her father and sister (554-55). But hers is the corrected version of Clytemnestra's story (555). She would speak ὀρθῶς 'in a straight way, correctly' and would speak not simply for Iphigenia, as her mother did, but for her father, too. She claims to be able to reconcile the two opposing elements of

Clytemnestra's story—the death of Iphigenia and the death of Agamemnon.

Clytemnestra then gives Electra permission to speak and even makes a comment on Electra's polite manner of address:

καὶ μὴν ἐφίημ᾽ · εἰ δέ μ᾽ ὧδ᾽ ἀεὶ λόγους
ἐξῆρχες, οὐκ ἂν ἦσθα λυπηρὰ κλύειν.

Electra 556-57

Certainly I permit you; if you always
started up your conversation thus, you would not be painful to hear.

With the word ἐξῆρχες 'started up' Clytemnestra uses a term that describes the action of a poet. It is the verb Archilochus uses when he boasts that he knows how to 'start up' (ἐξάρξαι) the dithyramb (F 120 West). Similarly, Aristotle uses it in the *Poetics* of those who 'lead off' the dithyramb (*Poetics* 1449 a11). Clytemnestra is describing Electra's way of 'starting up' her version, her story of the deaths of Iphigenia and Agamemnon.

In her very first lines Electra stresses speaking and stories:

καὶ δὴ λέγω σοι. πατέρα φῂς κτεῖναι. τίς ἂν
τούτου λόγος γένοιτ᾽ ἂν αἰσχίων ἔτι,
εἴτ᾽ οὖν δικαίως εἴτε μή; λέξω δέ σοι,
ὡς οὐ δίκῃ γ᾽ ἔκτεινας, ἀλλά σ᾽ ἔσπασεν
πειθὼ κακοῦ πρὸς ἀνδρός, ᾧ τανῦν ξύνει.

Electra 558-62

Well, then, I tell you. You say that you killed my father. What
speech could there be more shameful yet than this,
whether you did it justly or not? I will tell you
that you did not kill justly, but the persuasion
of that evil man, with whom you now live, drew you on.

The first line establishes the opposition of Electra's story to Clytemnestra's, 'I tell' (λέγω), 'you say' (φῄς). Each of the first three lines of Electra's speech has one or more words of speaking (λέγω 'I tell', φής 'you say' 558; λόγος 'speech' 559; λέξω 'I will tell' 560). The fourth line begins the sentence in which Electra gives her version of what led Clytemnestra to kill her husband. There are many motives that Electra might ascribe to Clytemnestra, the desire for revenge, for example, or fear of retribution from the husband she betrayed. But Electra puts the reason in one word placed emphatically at the beginning of the line: it was πειθώ 'persuasion' (562), 'the persuasion of that evil man' (πειθὼ κακοῦ πρὸς ἀνδρός). It was not hatred of Agamemnon, it was not love of Aegisthus. It was the power of Aegisthus' words that gave him power over Clytemnestra and, ultimately, over Agamemnon himself.

Electra proceeds to tell her version of the slaying of Iphigenia. She begins her tale,

πατήρ ποθ᾽ οὑμός, ὡς ἐγὼ κλύω,...

Electra 566

My father once, so I hear....

As has been observed, ὡς ἐγὼ κλύω 'so I hear' implies 'the possibility of other accounts'.[21] Electra is indicating that there are other accounts, but this is the version of the story that has authority for her. According to Electra, her father, when he had shot a stag, happened to utter a certain boast (ἐκκομπάσας ἔπος τι τυγχάνει βαλών 569), thus angering Artemis, who demanded the sacrifice of Agamemnon's daughter (570-73). As she did when she saw πειθώ 'persuasion' as the force that moved Clytemnestra to kill Agamemnon, so here Electra sees the spoken word as the pivotal part of the story: it was Agamemnon's chance boast, his **epos** 'word' (569), that inspired Artemis' demand for Iphigenia's death. Electra believes

---

[21] Jebb 1894 at line 566 of the *Electra*.

that particular story of the slaying of Iphigenia in which a word had power and Agamemnon had no choice.

Like Clytemnestra, who accused Electra of using the story of Agamemnon's death as a pretext for her criticism of her mother (525-26), Electra says that Clytemnestra is using the death of Iphigenia as a σκῆψις 'pretext' for the killing of Agamemnon (584). Electra asks Clytemnestra why, if her motive for killing Agamemnon was revenge for the death of her daughter, she now lives with her fellow murderer and rejects Agamemnon's children in favor of Aegisthus' (585-90). In the face of these actions, Electra says, she certainly cannot take the stance of the poet of praise:

πῶς ταῦτ' ἐπαινέσαιμ' ἄν;

Electra 591

How could I praise these things?

Nor can she take the stance of the blame poet:

ἀλλ' οὐ γὰρ οὐδὲ νουθετεῖν ἔξεστί σε,
ἣ πᾶσαν ἵης γλῶσσαν ὡς τὴν μητέρα
κακοστομοῦμεν.

Electra 595-97

But I may not reproach you,
who let loose your whole tongue, saying that
I speak badly of my mother.

According to Electra, if she tries to admonish Clytemnestra, using the language of blame (νουθετεῖν 'reproach' 595), then Clytemnestra retaliates by reproaching Electra for speaking ill of her mother (596-97). Clytemnestra is like Eurykleia, blaming another for the language of blame.

Clytemnestra proceeds to do exactly what Electra has predicted. After the chorus comment on Electra's speech

(610-11), Clytemnestra takes the stance of the blame poet and rebukes Electra for reproaching her mother:

ποίας δ' ἐμοὶ δεῖ πρός γε τήνδε φροντίδος,
ἥτις τοιαῦτα τὴν τεκοῦσαν ὕβρισεν,
καὶ ταῦτα τηλικοῦτος; ἀρά σοι δοκεῖ
χωρεῖν ἂν ἐς πᾶν ἔργον αἰσχύνης ἄτερ;

Electra 612-15

What sort of consideration should I have regarding this woman
who commits such outrages against the one who bore her,
and this at her age? Don't you think
that she would proceed to any deed without shame?

Each poet of blame finds the other's words a cause for rebuke. In this scene, the audience feels that the struggle of words between the two women is a continuous argument without resolution. Faced with a stalemate of blame and counter blame, Clytemnestra finally resorts to another power:

ἀλλ' οὐ μὰ τὴν δέσποιναν Ἄρτεμιν θράσους
τοῦδ' οὐκ ἀλύξεις, εὖτ' ἂν Αἴγισθος μόλῃ.

Electra 626-27

But, by the goddess Artemis, you will not escape
punishment for this insolence, when Aegisthus comes.

As Clytemnestra indicates, it will take the power and presence of a male authority figure, Aegisthus, to resolve the argument in Clytemnestra's favor. Clytemnestra is admitting that she herself is not able to establish her account of the past, or present, as true. She cannot control Electra and Electra's arguments by means of her own words—only Aegisthus has this power.

Clytemnestra then turns her attention to what initially brought her outside. She demands silence from Electra so that she can pray to Apollo as she makes her offerings to the god (630-31). Saying that she has come to ask Apollo for deliverance from her fears (634-36), Clytemnestra begins her prayer, constructed in the manner of a poem for the **sophoi**:

κλύοις ἂν ἤδη, Φοῖβε προστατήριε,
κεκρυμμένην μου βάξιν. οὐ γὰρ ἐν φίλοις
ὁ μῦθος, οὐδὲ πᾶν ἀναπτύξαι πρέπει
πρὸς φῶς παρούσης τῆσδε πλησίας ἐμοί,
μὴ σὺν φθόνῳ τε καὶ πολυγλώσσῳ βοῇ
σπείρῃ ματαίαν βάξιν εἰς πᾶσαν πόλιν.

Electra 637-42

You would hear now, Phoebus my protector,
a cryptic utterance [**baxis**] from me. For not among the near and dear is
my speech [**muthos**], nor is it appropriate for me to unfold everything
to the light while this one is near,
lest with envy and a full-voiced shout
she spread an idle rumor [**baxis**] to the whole city.

Clytemnestra's is a hidden utterance (638), one that her audience, Phoebus, would understand (637). As something hidden and meant for a special audience, Clytemnestra's prayer is reminiscent of another poet's comment on his own poetry:

ταῦτά μοι ᾐνίχθω κεκρυμμένα τοῖς ἀγαθοῖσιν.[22]

Theognis 681

Let these things be said as allusive words, hidden by me for noble men.

Clytemnestra assumes that Apollo is a member of her poetic community, one who correctly interprets her ambiguous message. Even the word she uses of her prayer, **baxis**, is a word of more than one meaning. It can be used in the elevated sense of an 'inspired oracular utterance', as it is used in the *Trachiniae* of the oracle concerning Heracles (87). Or it can be a simple report or rumor (e.g., Theognis 1298). Appearing first in her

---

[22] So cited by Jebb 1894 at line 638 of the *Electra*.

prayer in the sense of 'inspired utterance' (638), the word **baxis** puts her prayer, and herself, in the realm of prophecy and poetry. That the word **baxis** is ambiguous is emphasized when, just a few lines later, Clytemnestra speaks of the idle **baxis** 'rumor' that she fears Electra will spread (642). Clytemnestra contrasts her words, which are inspired, with Electra's, which, in Clytemnestra's view, are insubstantial talk. Hers, Clytemnestra is saying, is an inspired utterance that only Apollo can understand, while Electra's words are mere rumor, an unauthenticated report. Though she could not win the earlier argument with Electra and had to look to Aegisthus' return for its resolution, Clytemnestra still maintains that her words, not Electra's, are authoritative.

Clytemnestra calls her prayer a **muthos** (639), a word that can mean any kind of speech, including an artistic story or narrative.[23] By using it with the verb ἀναπτύξαι 'to unfold', the word for unfolding the rolls on which books are written,[24] Clytemnestra suggests that it is the literary kind of **muthos**. Her prayer is like a literary work, a special one, that must not be opened and revealed to all.

With the word **muthos** Clytemnestra takes a stance that is similar to Orestes'. She calls her prayer a **muthos** just as Orestes referred to his production, the story he has the Paidagogos tell, as a **muthos** ('let the **muthos** be established to this effect' 50). She has the right to speak things that are hidden because she is not among friends (638) and because she believes that she has a special understanding with Apollo (637-38). Similarly, in his first speech of the play, Orestes justified his use of deception on the basis of an oracle from Apollo (35-37). He too claims to have a special relationship with Apollo, one that only he and the **philoi** understand.

---

[23] For more on the word **muthos**, see Nagy 1989.3-22 and Martin 1989.
[24] As in Herodotus 1.125.2.

But Clytemnestra believes that her relationship with the god is such that she can even order Apollo to suit his way of hearing to her style of speech. She speaks in an allusive way (637-38) and instructs the god to listen accordingly:

ἀλλ᾽ ὧδ᾽ ἄκουε· τῇδε γὰρ κἀγὼ φράσω.

Electra 643

But listen in this way; for in this way also I shall speak.

Clytemnestra sees herself as the director who, by her manner of speaking, can control her audience, even the god himself.

Clytemnestra now gives the reason for her prayer: the dream of Agamemnon, which she refers to as φάσματα δισσῶν ὀνείρων 'visions of two-fold dreams' (644-45). With the phrase 'two-fold dreams' she is saying that the dream, like poetry, has two possible interpretations. In the context of her own ambiguous speech ('You would hear … a cryptic utterance from me' 637-38), she recognizes the ambiguous nature of her visions and prays accordingly:

εἰ μὲν πέφηνεν ἐσθλά, δὸς τελεσφόρα,
εἰ δ᾽ ἐχθρά, τοῖς ἐχθροῖσιν ἔμπαλιν μέθες.

Electra 646-47

If they have appeared as good visions, give them fulfillment,
if hateful, send them back upon my enemies.

She asks Apollo to protect her from treachery and to ensure her continued rule (648-54) and closes with the hope that Apollo will grant everything she requests (655-56). As for the things that she has left unspoken:

τὰ δ᾽ ἄλλα πάντα καὶ σιωπώσης ἐμοῦ
ἐπαξιῶ σε δαίμον᾽ ὄντ᾽ ἐξειδέναι·
τοὺς ἐκ Διὸς γὰρ εἰκός ἐστι πάνθ᾽ ὁρᾶν.

Electra 657-59

All other things, even though I am silent about them,
I expect you, being a god, to know;
for it is likely that the offspring of Zeus see all.

Clytemnestra expects Apollo to perceive without the medium of
words. Though she is silent, he will understand (657-58).
Clytemnestra thus claims a relationship to Apollo so close that
she does not need words, not even the language of the poet, to
communicate with him.

To Clytemnestra's plea for help and her claim of a special
relationship to the god, Apollo seems to provide an answer. At
the end of her prayer, a messenger arrives:

ξέναι γυναῖκες, πῶς ἂν εἰδείην σαφῶς
εἰ τοῦ τυράννου δώματ' Αἰγίσθου τάδε;

Electra 660-61

Gracious ladies, how might I know clearly
if this is the home of the ruler Aegisthus?

As has been observed, the Paidagogos' arrival at just this
moment is reminiscent of the *Oedipus Tyrannus* when Jocasta's
prayers to Apollo seem to be immediately answered by the
appearance of the messenger from Corinth (925).[25] In effect, the
Paidagogos is Apollo's answer to Clytemnestra's prayer. He
has come to carry out the order contained in Apollo's earlier
answer to Orestes, when the god instructed him,

ἄσκευον αὐτὸν ἀσπίδων τε καὶ στρατοῦ
δόλοισι κλέψαι χειρὸς ἐνδίκου σφαγάς.

Electra 36-37

without shields and army,
by means of deceptions, to seize the slaying of a just hand.

---

[25] See, for example, Reinhardt 1979.151.

To Clytemnestra's insistence that she has a special relationship with the god and to her plea for help, the appearance of the Paidagogos, the actor in Orestes' drama, is Apollo's answer. The special relationship with the god, the power of the **muthos**, belong, not to Clytemnestra, but to Orestes.

CHAPTER 3

The Play Begins

When the Paidagogos arrives in his role as messenger from Phocis, Clytemnestra has just described her dream of Agamemnon as φάσματα δισσῶν ὀνείρων 'visions of two-fold dreams' (644-45). Realizing that her 'visions' have two possible interpretations, she has prayed accordingly to Apollo (646-47).

The Paidagogos arrives with his own vision, the story of Orestes' death, a story that he claims to tell as an eyewitness (762-64). As soon as he comes on stage, the audience is struck by his new persona, for he is now two characters in one. In contrast to his first appearance, when he opened the play as Orestes' guide, pointing out all the landmarks of Mycenae (1-14), he now pretends to to be the newcomer who must ask the chorus for guidance (660-61).

The audience see the Paidagogos as a character who, like Clytemnestra's dreams, has two interpretations. His words and appearance are those of the messenger from Phocis and, at the same time, of the Paidagogos, teacher and friend of Orestes. The audience can interpret this messenger in two ways. They see and hear him in the same way that Clytemnestra does, but at the same time, since they are aware of his true identity, they know how to interpret both his appearance and his words correctly. They are the true **philoi** of the Paidagogos and Orestes.

The messenger/Paidagogos will now deliver an **ainos**, the story of Orestes' death, to Clytemnestra and to the audience of Sophocles' play. Using the **ainos** 'an allusive tale containing an ulterior purpose', the Paidagogos takes the role of the traditional poet, who speaks in ways that only those who are **philoi** 'near and dear', **agathoi** 'noble', and **sophoi** 'wise' can understand:[1]

> ταῦτά μοι ἠνίχθω κεκρυμμένα τοῖς ἀγαθοῖσιν.
> γινώσκοι δ᾽ ἄν τις καὶ κακὸν[2] ἄν σοφὸς ᾖ.

> Theognis 681-82

Let these things be said as allusive words, hidden by me for the **agathoi**. One could be aware even of an evil thing, if one is **sophos**.

If Clytemnestra were one of the **sophoi**, she might see the κακόν 'evil' that is to come. The Paidagogos tells her of it in the **ainos**, but she fails to interpret his words correctly. The real **sophoi** are the play's audience. The power and the attraction of Sophoclean irony for the audience is that it is inclusive. The audience are among the **sophoi** who, unlike Clytemnestra, understand the true meaning of the **ainos**. They feel the bond of **philotês** 'friendship' with the Paidagogos since he is the one

---

[1] For the **ainos** and its audience, see p. 3n4 and pp. 22-23 above.
[2] For a defense of the manuscript reading κακόν, see Nagy 1985.25.

who can communicate, and they are the ones who can interpret, the two-fold nature of his discourse.

The words of the messenger/Paidagogos are a special example of Sophoclean irony. Generally, when a character in Sophocles speaks words that are ironic, he says what he believes will have one effect on a character, while unknowingly producing another. The player does not himself realize the double nature of what he says, but the person to whom he speaks does. As noted, the messenger from Corinth in the *Oedipus Tyrannus* is similar to the Paidagogos in that he arrives as the apparent answer to a prayer.[3] Like the Paidagogos, too, he is a messenger bringing news of a death, in his case, the death of Polybus. In the case of the Corinthian messenger, though, the speaker of the ironic lines believes he is bearing good news and is unaware of the true import of what he says. However, his listener, Oedipus, understands. In the *Electra* the situation is reversed. The 'messenger' understands fully the double meaning of his story; his listener Clytemnestra does not. In the Paidagogos' performance, we see the playwright in action.[4] The Paidagogos is like the poet Sophocles, conscious of the irony of the story he creates and aware of its effect. In the Paidagogos we see the poet who intentionally uses ambiguous language and elicits a two-fold response: one from the on-stage character and one from his audience, the **philoi** who truly understand.

But Clytemnestra believes that she is one of the **philoi**, speaking to one of her own. Orestes has instructed the Paidagogos to say that he has been sent by Phanoteus of Phocis (44-45), and the Paidagogos accordingly does so (670). This

---

[3] See p. 85 above.

[4] For a discussion of the Paidagogos' messenger speech as a 'speech-act' and a very different view of the implications of his speech and Orestes' use of deception, see Kitzinger 1991.300 and 318-327.

identification of Phanoteus as the one who sends the news contrasts with that of Aeschylus, who says that it is Strophius who sends word of Orestes' death (*Choephoroe* 679). Phanoteus and Strophius are enemies representing opposite sides of a family feud.[5] Strophius, father of Pylades, had given Orestes a home in exile. As the enemy of Strophius, Phanoteus is represented by the Paidagogos as the friend of Clytemnestra who sends the 'good' news that Orestes is dead. Hearing that it is Phanoteus who sends him, Clytemnestra immediately recognizes the Paidagogos as one of her **philoi**, as she questions him about the sort of news he brings:

τὸ ποῖον, ὦ ξέν'; εἰπέ. παρὰ <u>φίλου</u> γὰρ ὢν
ἀνδρός, σάφ' οἶδα, <u>προσφιλεῖς</u> λέξεις λόγους.

Electra 671-72

What sort, my guest? Speak. Being from a <u>friendly</u> [philos]
man, as I clearly know, you will speak <u>friendly</u> [prosphileis] words.

Stressing its significance, Clytemnestra uses two forms of the adjective **philos** 'near and dear, friendly'. She assumes that both the Paidagogos and his message are 'friendly' to her. With his next words the Paidagogos fulfills Clytemnestra's expectations, delivering the most welcome message of all:

τέθνηκ' Ὀρέστης· ἐν βραχεῖ ξυνθεὶς λέγω.

Electra 673

Orestes is dead; summing it up in brief, I tell you.

With this news, Clytemnestra is sure that she is listening to one of the **philoi** and that she and the Paidagogos/messenger are in sympathy with one another. Clytemnestra sees herself as part of a community that includes the Paidagogos.

---

5 See Jebb 1894 at line 45 of the *Electra* and Kells 1973 at lines 44f.

With the words ἐν βραχεῖ ξυνθεὶς λέγω 'summing it up in brief, I tell you' (673), the Paidagogos makes a comment about story telling. He says that he is relating the short version of his story. The verb συντίθημι 'to sum up' literally means 'put together' and is used in the sense of 'composing' works of art. As such it is used, for example, in Plato of composing μῦθοι 'stories' (*Republic* 377d), ποίησις 'poetry' (*Phaedrus* 278c), μελῳδία 'choral song' (*Laws* 812d), and ὄρχησις 'dance' (*Laws* 816c). The Paidagogos is aware of two ways of 'composing' a story—ἐν βραχεῖ 'in brief' or the elaborate, Homeric version which he will proceed to give. Like a fifth-century playwright, he has received certain parameters of the story, but now he is to decide the exact way in which the tale will be told.

Electra's response to the Paidagogos' report is a cry of lament, but Clytemnestra cuts her off:

HΛ. οἲ 'γὼ τάλαιν᾽, ὄλωλα τῇδ᾽ ἐν ἡμέρᾳ.
KΛ. τί φής, τί φής, ὦ ξεῖνε; μὴ ταύτης κλύε.

Electra 674-75

El. Alas, I am wretched, I have perished on this day.
Cl. What are you saying, what are you saying, my guest? Don't listen to her!

Clytemnestra takes the role of director and composer, trying to control the speech of those around her. She prompts the Paidagogos: τί φής, τί φής; 'What are you saying, what are you saying?' She cuts off Electra: μὴ ταύτης κλύε 'Don't listen to her!' She directs the Paidagogos to speak while at the same time trying to deprive Electra of her audience. She tries to control both what the Paidagogos says and what he hears. Clytemnestra has the illusion that the Paidagogos is to her what he actually is to Orestes: a player, one of the **philoi** whom the director can control. When she prompts her player (675), insisting that he repeat the news, the Paidagogos responds accordingly:

θανόντ' 'Ορέστην νῦν τε καὶ τότ' ἐννέπω.[6]

Electra 676

Orestes is dead, I tell you now as I did then.

The verb the Paidagogos uses for the 'telling' of his tale of Orestes, ἐννέπω, is one used of the very famous telling of the tale of Odysseus: ἄνδρα μοι ἔννεπε, Μοῦσα, πολύτροπον 'Tell me, Muse, of the man of many ways' (*Odyssey* 1.1). The choice of this verb is already a hint that his message is more than a simple report from Phanoteus. The Paidagogos is about to tell a tale, using the language of epic, about Orestes, a man very much like Odysseus, a king who uses disguise and deception to re-establish his authority and regain his home.

To the Paidagogos' second announcement of Orestes' death, Electra responds with another cry of despair (677). Again Clytemnestra dismisses her and urges the Paidagogos to speak:

σὺ μὲν τὰ σαυτῆς πρᾶσσ', ἐμοὶ δὲ σύ, ξένε,
τἀληθὲς εἰπέ, τῷ τρόπῳ διόλλυται;

Electra 678-79

You, see to your own affairs, but you, my guest,
tell me the truth: how did he die?

Clytemnestra indicates that she does not simply want the 'short version' (ἐν βραχεῖ 673) of the story. She wishes to know the 'truth' (679), and the details: 'How did he die?' (τῷ τρόπῳ διόλλυται; 679). Here she actually uses the vivid historic present: 'How does he die?' as though demanding the immediacy of an eyewitness account. To her request to hear the

---

[6] Here I follow the reading of Pearson 1924 and Kells 1973. The manuscripts include both ἐννέπω and λέγω.

detailed version of the story, the Paidagogos responds truthfully:

κἀπεμπόμην πρὸς ταῦτα καὶ τὸ πᾶν φράσω.

Electra 680

I was sent for this and I will tell the whole story.

In fact, Orestes did send the Paidagogos to tell the story of his death. With Clytemnestra's prompting, the Paidagogos is now about to begin his longer, Homeric version of the story. In his directions to the Paidagogos (47), Orestes may have instructed his player to tell the elaborate version of the story, the one with **ogkos** 'padding'.[7] As one critic comments on the Paidagogos' description of the chariot race and Orestes' death:

> The Paedagogus may have been told by Orestes to add **ogkos** (bulk, embroidery, ornamentation) to the simple announcement that 'Orestes is dead'....This narrative shows him doing it brilliantly.[8]

Ready to tell τὸ πᾶν, the 'whole' story, adding **ogkos** to the tale, the Paidagogos begins his more elaborate account, immediately introducing Orestes into the narrative:

κεῖνος γὰρ ἐλθὼν ἐς τὸ κλεινὸν Ἑλλάδος
πρόσχημ᾽ ἀγῶνος Δελφικῶν ἄθλων χάριν,

Electra 681-82

That man, having come to Greece's renowned ornament [**proskhêma**] of a contest [**agôn**], for the Delphian competitions ....

As the scholia and later critics have pointed out, Orestes' choice (49) of the Pythian games as the scene of his death is an anachronism.[9] The Pythian games were originally not contests

---

[7] For discussion of this passage, see pp. 30-31 above.
[8] Kells 1973 at introduction to lines 680-763 of the *Electra*.
[9] Jebb 1894 at lines 48ff. and Kamerbeek 1974 at line 49 of the *Electra*.

of athletics, but contests of music and poetry celebrated in honor of Apollo. Even after athletic contests were introduced, the μουσικοί 'musical and poetic' contests were still the first of the day. They were then followed by the athletic contests in the order in which the Paidagogos will present them: the γυμνικοὶ ἀγῶνες 'gymnastic contests', which included the footrace, and then the ἱππικοί 'equestrian' competitions, which included the chariot race.[10]

It has been said that this anachronism is one to which "Attic Tragedy was wholly indifferent."[11] But the choice is a matter not of indifference, but of significance. The Paidagogos is telling an **ainos** that only he and the audience of the *Electra* understand. As he presents the fiction of the chariot race, the Paidagogos is simultaneously telling the truth: Orestes has entered into an **agôn** 'contest' not of athletics, but into one that, like the original Pythian games, is a contest of music and poetry. Orestes is putting on a dramatic production, and his featured player, the Paidagogos, now tells the true nature of the contest in an **ainos** to an uncomprehending Clytemnestra.

The Paidagogos calls the competition at Delphi not simply an **agôn**, but the **proskhêma** of an **agôn** (682). The word **proskhêma** can mean an 'ornament', and the phrase τὸ κλεινὸν Ἑλλάδος πρόσχημ' ἀγῶνος has been translated as 'Greece's famous show-piece [proskhêma] of a contest [agôn]'.[12] But as we have seen,[13] the fundamental meaning of the word **proskhêma**, related to the verb προέχω, means 'that which is held forth', and can mean 'that which is held before to cover,

---

[10] Jebb 1894 at line 683, who cites Plutarch *Quaestiones Convivales* 2.4.
[11] Jebb 1894 at lines 48ff. of the *Electra*.
[12] Kells 1973 at lines 681ff. of the *Electra*.
[13] See pp. 75-76 above.

screen, cloak'.[14] Clytemnestra has already used this word in the sense of 'pretext': in her argument with her daughter, she complained that Electra was speaking ill of her (523-24) and then continued: πατὴρ γάρ, οὐδὲν ἄλλο, σοὶ πρόσχημ᾽ ἀεί 'your father—and nothing else—that's always your pretext [proskhêma]'. The story of Agamemnon's death, according to Clytemnestra, is nothing but a proskhêma 'pretext' for Electra's criticisms of her mother. Clytemnestra is, then, quite aware of the use of the word proskhêma as 'screen' and of the use of the word with reference to a story that she considers untrue, namely, Electra's version of the death of Agamemnon.

Addressing Clytemnestra, the Paidagogos here uses the word proskhêma in the two senses of the word. To those who, like Clytemnestra, are not the philoi, the term 'proskhêma of an agôn' simply means 'show-piece of a contest'. But for himself and the audience, the true philoi, he is using the word in exactly the same way that Clytemnestra did. He is telling Clytemnestra that what he is presenting is a 'screen' in the form of a fictitious story. When he uses the term 'proskhêma of an agôn', he means a 'screen consisting of a contest' in the sense that the whole story of the athletic games is a way of covering up Orestes' true identity. The fictitious contest of the Pythian games obscures the fact that Orestes is still alive.

The phrase 'proskhêma of an agôn' can also mean 'a screen obscuring the contest', and the Paidagogos uses it in this way also. The story of Orestes' death is a means of covering up the fact that there is a contest going on at the moment of the Paidagogos' speech, a contest not of athletics, but of words and music. Like the original Pythian games, Orestes' is a game of

---

[14] For these two aspects to the word proskhêma and its use here and at *Electra* 525, but with a very different view of the word's significance, see Segal 1981.282-83.

music and poetry, a contest of artists in which he competes against Aegisthus and Clytemnestra.

The artistic struggle against Clytemnestra and Aegisthus is not simply one of music and poetry. It involves as well the visual aspects of the drama. The word **proskhêma** is used of the 'pomp' of tragedy (Aristophanes *Frogs* 912-13) and, in this sense, reflects Orestes' use of sight as well as sound. Orestes is using the appearance of the Paidagogos, his ability to play convincingly the part of the messenger and to make the audience believe, by his expressions and gestures, that what he says is true. Just as the Pythian games are a 'show-piece of a contest', so this 'messenger' speech of the Paidagogos is the 'show-piece' of Orestes' play.

The Paidagogos proceeds to describe Orestes' entrance in the footrace:

εἰσῆλθε λαμπρός, πᾶσι τοῖς ἐκεῖ σέβας·

Electra 685

He came in, radiant, a thing of awe for all who were there ….

With the term εἰσῆλθε 'he came in' the Paidagogos uses the verb that is the technical term for 'taking one's place' in a contest.[15] The verb is also used of the chorus and actors when they make their entrance and 'come upon' the stage (Plato *Republic* 580b and Xenophon *Anabasis* 6.1.9). While describing a fictitious contest of athletics, the Paidagogos describes what is actually happening at the moment he speaks. A player, the Paidagogos, has both come on stage and entered into the competition.

The Paidagogos tells of Orestes' victory in the footrace (686-87) and again makes reference to his own technique of story telling. Just as he commented on his own terse

---

[15] Demosthenes 18.319, as cited by Jebb 1894 and Kells 1973 at line 685 of the *Electra*.

announcement that Orestes was dead by using the term ἐν βραχεῖ ξυνθεὶς λέγω 'summing it up in brief, I tell you' (673), so now he says that he cannot include all the details. There is much to tell, but the Paidagogos must limit himself to the main points of the story:

> χὤπως μὲν ἐν παύροισι πολλά σοι λέγω,
> οὐκ οἶδα τοιοῦδ' ἀνδρὸς ἔργα καὶ κράτη·

Electra 688-89

And how I am to tell you in a few words the many
deeds and powers of such a man, I do not know.

The Paidagogos comments on the difficulty of telling his story, and by thus drawing attention to his own role as storyteller, he hints of his true nature to Clytemnestra.

When the Paidagogos says that there was no one who surpassed Orestes in ἔργα 'deeds' and 'powers' κράτη (689), he is telling Clytemnestra about the true character of Orestes.[16] At the end of the prologue the Paidagogos had encouraged Orestes and Pylades by telling them that their actions would bring νίκη 'victory' and κράτος τῶν δρωμένων 'power over the things being done' (85). By telling Clytemnestra that Orestes is the victor who is superior to all others, he accurately describes Orestes' nature and predicts his ultimate triumph over Aegisthus and Clytemnestra.

The Paidagogos has admitted that he cannot tell all the details of Orestes' victories in the games, but he insists that Clytemnestra 'be aware of one thing' (ἓν δ' ἴσθι 690). Of the many contests that were announced,

---

[16] See Benveniste 1969.71-83 vol. 2 for κράτος 'power' meaning 'supériorité, prévalence' and signifying both the power of the warrior and the authority of the king.

τούτων ἐνεγκὼν πάντα τἀπινίκια,
ὠλβίζετ᾽,

Electra 692

of these he gained all the prizes [epinikia] and
was considered blessed ....

As has been observed, the word **epinikia** that the
Paidagogos uses for 'prizes' usually means either 'the songs of
victory' or, with ἱερά understood, a 'sacrifice in honour of
victory'.[17] The word is used here in this unusual way, because
the Paidagogos, who is part of a dramatic competition, is
interested in the song of victory. With the phrase 'he gained all
the **epinikia**' the Paidagogos gives two pictures of Orestes.
One, which Clytemnestra sees, is the portrayal of Orestes as the
man who wins the victories in the athletic contests of the
Pythian games. But taking **epinikia** in its usual sense of 'the
songs of victory' in turn changes the sense of the verb φέρω with
which it is used, rendering 'bringing the victory songs'. In this
sense it is similar to a phrase in the opening lines of a very
famous victory song concerning the Pythian games, φέρων μέλος
ἔρχομαι 'I come bringing this song' (Pindar *Pythian* 2.3-4).

With this second sense of 'bringing the victory song', the
Paidagogos describes what Orestes is doing at the very moment
that he, the Paidagogos, speaks. Orestes is bringing a victory
song to Mycenae, and the messenger speech is a part of it.
Orestes' victory song is the play that he himself creates, the
play that brings victory, victory over Clytemnestra and
Aegisthus. Like the struggles of the athletic games, the words
and visions of the drama that Orestes presents, the
performance that he and the Paidagogos give, are part of a
competitive struggle. The Paidagogos, in relating the fiction of

---

[17] Jebb 1894 at line 692 of the *Electra*.

an athletic **agôn**, is in fact telling of and performing in a dramatic **agôn**. At the same time, the audience, the **philoi** who understand the underlying message of the **ainos,** cannot help but be aware that this dramatic **agôn,** this competition between rival playwrights, is being performed in the context of a dramatic competition, the City Dionysia.

The Paidagogos is like the fifth-century playwright, who, having received a story, considers how to tell it. Like the Athenian dramatist, the Paidagogos decides what elements of the story to focus on: 'how I am to tell you in a few words...'(688). He is well aware that his composition and presentation are part of a competitive effort, in this case, one against Clytemnestra and Aegisthus. In this way he mirrors what the fifth-century playwright does, what, in fact, Sophocles has done in choosing which aspects of the Orestes story to focus on and in entering his version of the story in a dramatic festival.

Not only does the Paidagogos use **epinikia** in the sense of 'victory song', but he also uses the word in its other sense of 'sacrifice in honor of the victory'. For with his victory song Orestes will gain a sacrifice in the form of the deaths of Clytemnestra and Aegisthus.

The Paidagogos concludes his story of Orestes' winning all the prizes by telling of the announcement of his name as victor (693-95). It takes three lines to name Orestes, and there are three elements to his identity: he is an Argive, his name is Orestes, and he is the son of Agamemnon. Of these three aspects of his identity, the third, final, and most elaborately presented is his relationship to his father:

ὠλβίζετ᾽, Ἀργεῖος μὲν ἀνακαλούμενος,
ὄνομα δ᾽ Ὀρέστης, τοῦ τὸ κλεινὸν Ἑλλάδος
Ἀγαμέμνονος στράτευμ᾽ ἀγείραντός ποτε.

Electra 693-95

he was considered blessed, proclaimed an Argive,
Orestes by name, son of Agamemnon who once
gathered the renowned host of Greece.

These lines, which stress Orestes' relationship to his father, recall the very first words of the play. The Paidagogos addressed Orestes, identifying him as the son of Agamemnon:

ὦ τοῦ στρατηγήσαντος ἐν Τροίᾳ ποτὲ
᾽Αγαμέμνονος παῖ,

Electra 1-2

Son of Agamemnon who once led the army at Troy....

It is as though the play is beginning again, and for Clytemnestra it is. The deception, in the form of the messenger speech, is the beginning of the play that Orestes is producing. What we have seen until now is the preparation, the rehearsal. Now begins the play itself, the drama—the action of words—in which Clytemnestra becomes audience, participant, and sacrificial victim.

The Paidagogos has begun the new play by presenting a fictitious Orestes who is very much like the real man: the man of power and control, who wins every contest he undertakes. As one critic remarks:

And yet even this false Orestes whose death is announced, an Orestes surrounded by an aura of fame, victory and sport, must resemble the real Orestes to some extent, for both the real and the fictitious Orestes...think only of fame and victory.[18]

The Paidagogos, by presenting true facets of Orestes' character, continues to tell Clytemnestra an **ainos**, the true import of which she fails to comprehend.

[18]   Reinhardt 1979.152.

Having described Orestes as a man of power who repeatedly achieves victory, the Paidagogos proceeds to the crucial part of the deception, the fatal chariot race:

κεῖνος γὰρ ἄλλης ἡμέρας, ὅθ᾽ ἱππικῶν
ἦν ἡλίου τέλλοντος ὠκύπους ἀγών,
εἰσῆλθε πολλῶν ἁρματηλατῶν μέτα.

Electra 698-700

That man, on another day, when,
as the sun rose, it was time for the swift chariot contest,
came in with many charioteers.

As he did in the description of Orestes entering the first contest, the footrace (685), the Paidagogos now uses the verb εἰσῆλθε 'came in' to describe Orestes taking his position at the start of the chariot race. As noted, this verb is the one used both of athletes taking their positions in the contest and of actors coming on stage.[19] Just as the dramatic festival begins at dawn, so too does this contest of chariots begin with the sun rising (699). Again, just as the reference to Agamemnon reminded us of the opening of the play, so also does the reference to the dawn. In the opening scene of the play, the Paidagogos urged Orestes and Pylades to take counsel quickly, giving as his reason:

ὡς ἡμὶν ἤδη λαμπρὸν ἡλίου σέλας
ἑῷα κινεῖ φθέγματ᾽ ὀρνίθων σαφῆ,
μέλαινά τ᾽ ἄστρων ἐκλέλοιπεν εὐφρόνη.

Electra 17-19

Already for us the bright light of the sun
rouses the clear, early morning voices of birds
and the dark night of stars has gone.

[19] See p. 96 above.

Like the dramatic festival, like Orestes' return to Mycenae, the fictitious and fatal chariot race begins with the coming of dawn.

With his introduction to the chariot race, the Paidagogos indicates that he is relating a contest not only of chariots, but also of dramatics. In the story of the race itself there are hints of the true nature of both Orestes and the contest in which he is engaged. According to the Paidagogos' account of the race (709-48), one of the charioteers loses control of his horses and swerves, crashing into another team. The charioteer behind the crash, characterized as a **deinos** 'clever' man, pulls his team aside and lets those behind him go past, and these chariots cannot swerve out of the way of the accident ahead. With these contestants lost, only two are left in the race, Orestes and the **deinos** man who had the presence of mind to pull out of the way at the sight of the crash. The race between the two comes to an end when Orestes, drawing too close for the turn, catches the inside wheel on the turning-post and is hurled to his death from the chariot.

In his description of the chariot race, the Paidagogos suggests something about the real Orestes. The fictitious Orestes is the contestant who has been holding back (734-35), 'putting his trust in the end' (τῷ τέλει πίστιν φέρων 735). We are reminded of the real Orestes, who did not care whether he died in story, as long as he was 'saved in deed' (59-60). Like the fictitious charioteer, who seems to be losing as he holds back his team and puts his trust in the end, so, as the Paidagogos speaks, the real Orestes seems to have lost in the competition with Clytemnestra and Aegisthus. In fact, Orestes has, as he said earlier, confidence that he will emerge from the telling of the story of his death, like a star, shining on his enemies:

ὡς κἄμ' ἐπαυχῶ τῆσδε τῆς φήμης ἄπο
δεδορκότ' ἐχθροῖς ἄστρον ὣς λάμψειν ἔτι.

Electra 65-66

So I am confident that from this story I,
alive, shall yet shine upon my enemies like a star.

By reducing the race to a contest between just two drivers, Orestes and the **deinos** charioteer, the messenger/Paidagogos hints at the real contest in Mycenae: a contest between two clever men, Aegisthus and Orestes. In his description of the end of the race, the Paidagogos emphasizes that the struggle is between just two men by using the dual as he vividly depicts them running neck and neck:

κἀξισώσαντε ζυγὰ
ἠλαυνέτην, τότ᾽ ἄλλος, ἄλλοθ᾽ ἅτερος
κάρα προβάλλων ἱππικῶν ὀχημάτων.

Electra 738-40

and the two brought the teams abreast
and they both drove on, first one, then the other
getting his head in front of the horse-drawn chariots.

When the Paidagogos tells of the spectators' reaction to the sight of Orestes thrown from the chariot and dragged by his horses, the word he uses of their cry of pity is ἀνωλόλυξε (**anôloluxe**) 'cried out' (750), a verb that is generally used of a shout for joy.[20] The double meaning of the word is appropriate here, for the moment of despair in the story of Orestes' fall is the moment of triumph for the Paidagogos, the storyteller who has vividly and convincingly told the tale of Orestes' death. Like the fictitious Orestes who moves the spectators to cry out, the Paidagogos moves his audience as he reaches the climax of his narration. With the ambiguous **anôloluxe** he captures the

[20] Jebb 1894 at lines 749ff. of the *Electra*. As is apparent from the discussion that follows, I see no reason to deviate from the manuscript reading of ἀνωλόλυξε, as do Lloyd-Jones and Wilson 1990a and 1990b, who adopt Herwerden's ἀνωτότυξε 'broke out into wailing'. Jebb 1894, Pearson 1924, Kells 1973, Kamerbeek 1974, and Dawe 1984 all keep the manuscript reading.

double nature of the moment—the despair of the story, the triumph of the storyteller.

The Paidagogos presents his final picture of Orestes, as men untangle his body from the reins in which he was caught:

ἔλυσαν αἱματηρόν, ὥστε μηδένα
γνῶναι φίλων ἰδόντ᾽ ἂν ἄθλιον δέμας.

Electra 755-56

They freed him, so bloodied that no one
of his **philoi**, seeing his tormented body, would recognize him.

None of the **philoi** could recognize him. Thus the purpose of the Paidagogos' story is successfully accomplished: Orestes in Mycenae is as he was in fiction—unrecognizable to anyone of the 'near and dear'. The blood of death covers him in fiction, as the fiction itself covers and protects him in life. The story of his death is Orestes' most effective disguise.

The Paidagogos then tells of the burning of the body:

καί νιν πυρᾷ κέαντες εὐθὺς <u>ἐν βραχεῖ</u>
χαλκῷ μέγιστον σῶμα δειλαίας σποδοῦ
φέρουσιν ἄνδρες Φωκέων τεταγμένοι,
ὅπως πατρῴας τύμβον ἐκλάχῃ χθονός.

Electra 757-60

And right away they burned him on the pyre, and <u>in a small</u>
[**en brakhei**] bronze vessel, they are bringing the very large body,
consisting of sad ash; appointed men of Phocis are bringing it,
so that he may have a tomb in his paternal land.

The large body is contained ἐν βραχεῖ χαλκῷ 'in a small bronze' vessel (757-58). We recall the Paidagogos' comment on his announcement of Orestes' death, that he was summing up the story 'in short', ἐν βραχεῖ ξυνθεὶς λέγω (673), where he used the same words **en brakhei** for 'in brief' as he does in this passage for 'in a small' bronze. We recall also his remark during the narration of Orestes' fictitious exploits, that he was trying to tell many things in a few words (ἐν παύροισι πολλά σοι λέγω 688). He has claimed that he is trying to put a long story into a short account.

The urn is here described in a way similar to that of the narration—a small thing that contains a large body. Later, when Orestes claims to be bearing the urn with Orestes' ashes, he uses, as does the Paidagogos here, the same expression, **en brakhei**, in exactly the same position at the end of the line:

φέροντες αὐτοῦ σμικρὰ λείψαν᾿ <u>ἐν βραχεῖ</u>
τεύχει θανόντος, ὡς ὁρᾷς, κομίζομεν.

Electra 1113-14

Bearing the scanty remains of the dead man <u>in a small</u> [**en brakhei**] urn, as you see, we bring him home.

Like the narration of the messenger speech that has been performed by the Paidagogos, the urn, first described as a τύπωμα χαλκόπλευρον 'bronze-sided casting' (54), is a work of art.[21] The work of art, the urn cast in bronze, is a small vessel containing the fiction of the unrecognizable body, just as the Paidagogos' work of art, the messenger speech, contains Orestes in disguise. The funeral urn is the physical aspect of the deception, as the Paidagogos' announcement is the verbal.

In the verbal part of the deception, the messenger speech itself, the Paidagogos uses the language of epic.[22] As commentators have pointed out, the description of the chariot race owes much to the account of the chariot race in the funeral games for Patroclus (*Iliad* 23.271 ff.).[23] In the first few lines of the Paidagogos' description of the race, we hear the sound of this epic tone:

[21] For discussion of the urn as a work of art, see pp. 32-35 above.
[22] See Davidson 1989.65-67 for the examples cited here.
[23] Jebb 1894, Kells 1973, Kamerbeek 1974 at lines 680-763 of the *Electra*, and Davidson 1989.65-67.

χαλκῆς ὑπαὶ σάλπιγγος ἦξαν· οἱ δ᾽ ἅμα
ἵπποις ὁμοκλήσαντες ἡνίας χεροῖν
ἔσεισαν· ἐν δὲ πᾶς ἐμεστώθη δρόμος
κτύπου κροτητῶν ἁρμάτων·

Electra 711-14

at the sound of the bronze trumpet they started up; they
shouted together at the horses and shook the reins
in their hands; the whole course was filled with
the noise of rattling chariots ....

Here we find the epic ὑπαί 'at the sound of' for the usual ὑπό
(711). Similarly, the verb used of shouting at the horses,
ὁμοκλήσαντες (712), is a word of epic and is, in fact, used in the
Iliad at the beginning of the description of the chariot race (*Iliad*
23.363). The use of this epic verb is the only such occurrence in
all tragedy.[24] The word used to describe the 'rattling' chariots,
κροτητῶν, derives from the epic κείν᾽ ὄχεα κροτέοντες (*Iliad*
15.453).

These and the many other expressions from epic are the
ogkos 'bulk' that Orestes may have asked the Paidagogos to
add when he instucted him regarding the messenger speech
(47).[25] The epic coloring is part of the **ogkos** that gives the story
breadth. When Orestes uses the Paidagogos as his actor and
poet, he is using the poetic style of an older poet, adopting the
language of his predecessor, the language of epic, and incorporating it into an artistic creation of his own, the drama.

As we recall, Sophocles himself is said to have described
his earlier style as one modelled on that of his predecessor,
Aeschylus, and he is reported to have used for the earliest stage

---

24 Davidson 1989.65-66.
25 See pp. 30-31 and 93 above.

of his own style the word **ogkos**.[26] It has been observed of the messenger speech that,

> Sophocles has permitted himself in this speech of intrigue a kind of diction which as a tragic writer he had probably long abandoned for serious material. It is as though he were playing a game with his own earlier tragic style.[27]

Orestes does with the Paidagogos' speech what Sophocles himself is doing as creator of this scene—incorporating an 'old-fashioned' style into a very contemporary production.

In the telling of the story of the chariot race, we see how drama takes over the language of another genre and makes it a part of its own. The language of epic has now become part of a medium that is not only verbal, but visual (note again the semantics of **theatron** 'theater' from **theaomai** 'see'). Language now has the medium of the actor, the power of his presence and narration, the illusion of his disguise.

Clytemnestra is completely convinced by the Paidagogos' performance and narration. The only question in her mind is what words she should choose in response:

ὦ Ζεῦ, τί ταῦτα, πότερον εὐτυχῆ λέγω,
ἢ δεινὰ μέν, κέρδη δέ; λυπηρῶς δ᾽ ἔχει,
εἰ τοῖς ἐμαυτῆς τὸν βίον σῴζω κακοῖς.

Electra 766-68

Zeus, what about these things? Should I say they are fortunate,
or terrible, but profitable [**kerdos**]? It is grievous,
if I save my life by my own evils.

We note in Clytemnestra's speech here the many verbal echoes of Orestes' words near the beginning of the play, when he spoke of the deceptive story of the chariot race:

---

26 See pp. 20-21 above.
27 Reinhardt 1979.151.

108   *Chapter 3*

τί γάρ με λυπεῖ τοῦθ', ὅταν λόγῳ θανὼν
ἔργοισι σωθῶ κἀξενέγκωμαι κλέος;
δοκῶ μέν, οὐδὲν ῥῆμα σὺν κέρδει κακόν.

Electra 59-61

For what does it grieve me, when, dying in word,
I am saved by deeds and gain glory?
I think that no word, with profit [**kerdos**], is bad.

Orestes was considering words—the very words which
Clytemnestra is now reacting to—with **kerdos** 'profit'. His
mother thinks that she is talking about deeds (the death of
Orestes) which are **kerdos** for her (767), when in fact she is
talking about words which are **kerdos** for Orestes and which
will prove most unprofitable for herself. In using the word
kerdos, the word that also designates the 'craft' of poetry,
Clytemnestra is unwittingly accurate: the words of the
Paidagogos are **kerdos**, profit through poetic craft.[28]

The craft of the messenger speech gives Orestes' story a
power that surpasses the stories of others. In the scene prior to
the messenger speech (516-633), Clytemnestra and Electra each
struggled to establish her own version of the story of the death
of Agamemnon as true. Taking the stance of the poet, each used
the traditional language of praise and blame in a struggle of
conflicting versions of the past. But without a male authority to
establish one story as true, neither woman could overcome the
other. The Paidagogos, by virtue of his disguise as the
messenger of Phanoteus and by the power of his narrative
skills, is able to convince both women that his false story is
true.

The Paidagogos' narrative is preceded by the conflicting
stories of two women, Clytemnestra and Electra, and similarly,

---

[28] For discussion of Orestes' words (lines 59-66) and **kerdos** as poetic
craft, see pp. 35-38 above.

it is followed by conflicting stories of two women, Electra and Chrysothemis (871-937). In the next scene Chrysothemis, having observed offerings at Agamemnon's tomb, tells Electra that she has seen proof that Orestes has returned. Electra, convinced by the Paidagogos' story that Orestes is dead, in turn persuades Chrysothemis of the truth of the Paidagogos' story and the falseness of Chrysothemis'. Despite the fact that Chrysothemis tells the true story and the Paidagogos tells the false, his version is accepted rather than hers. Fiction, as created and told by the Paidagogos, has more power than truth.[29]

The messenger speech is a triumph of fiction over other fictions and over the truth itself. It is the beginning of the triumph of Orestes and the Paidagogos over Clytemnestra and Aegisthus. Clytemnestra believes the Paidagogos' words and acts on them. She enters into the drama of Orestes and is a participant, playing the part that he has designed for her. Confident because of his words, she feels that she is now in charge. Believing that she is the director, she now decides who will go off stage, who will stay on. The Paidagogos politely offers to leave (799),[30] but Clytemnestra insists that he come inside as a guest and that Electra stay outside:

ἀλλ᾽ εἴσιθ᾽ εἴσω· τήνδε δ᾽ ἔκτοθεν βοᾶν
ἔα τά θ᾽ αὑτῆς καὶ τὰ τῶν φίλων κακά.

Electra 802-3

But come in; leave this one outside to shout out
her troubles and those of her **philoi**.

---

[29] Compare the power of Odysseus' fiction in the *Philoctetes*. For discussion, see Greengard 1987.26-27.

[30] Note that Clytemnestra dismisses the idea of his leaving with ἥκιστα 'not at all' (800), the very same word with which the Paidagogos dismissed Orestes' suggestion of staying to listen to Electra, when, at the beginning of the play, the Paidagogos controlled the scene. See pp. 42-44 above.

Unlike the woman who had, as Chrysothemis indicated (379-82), planned to imprison Electra and silence her forever, Clytemnestra now feels so in control of the situation that she does not fear to leave Electra outside 'shouting' out her troubles. With the word βοᾶν 'to shout' she indicates that once again she sees Electra as the inarticulate and, thus, powerless mourner. Now Clytemnestra enters the house just as she has entered the illusions of Orestes' drama. She is confident in her apparent triumph, and this confidence is the measure of the totality of her defeat. She enters into the play and into the house, the house that is to be the site and scene of her final performance, the stage for her own death, as she becomes the sacrificial victim to the avenging hero.

CHAPTER 4

The Final Contest

With its shifts between illusion and reality, the *Electra* gives its audience a view of the artist as he creates the drama. As we have seen, the opening scene is the rehearsal of Orestes' drama, as he directs the Paidagogos on how to play his part for the great messenger scene.[1] When the Paidagogos delivers the messenger speech, the audience has made the transition from the rehearsal of the play to the presentation of the drama itself. The high point of Orestes' production is the messenger speech, in which his chief player, the Paidagogos, creates a fiction more powerful and compelling than the truth itself.[2]

The recognition of Orestes by Electra (1098-1325) is the first in a series of recognition scenes that end the play. After

[1] See Chapter 1.
[2] See Chapter 3.

this scene there follows another in which Electra realizes that the messenger from Phocis is actually the Paidagogos (1326-75). When Aegisthus comes on stage, he has two moments of recognition. First, when he draws the veil away from the body that has been brought on stage, he discovers, not the body of Orestes, as he had expected, but the body of Clytemnestra. That moment of recognition leads immediately to another, as he realizes that the man he is addressing must be, not a messenger from Phocis, but the man whose corpse he had expected to see, Orestes. The play moves repeatedly from illusion to reality as the characters around Orestes discover the truth behind the appearance.

The recognition scenes at the end of the play bring us back again to the reality behind the illusion: Electra and Aegisthus each see who the strangers from Phocis truly are. But reality has been changed by fiction. When the Paidagogos and Orestes appeared at the beginning of the play, they were the powerless outsiders; Aegisthus and Clytemnestra were the authority figures. Now, because of the power of the drama that he has created, directed, and presented, Orestes gains control over Clytemnestra, Aegisthus, and Mycenae.

The final scenes of the play are not only a movement from illusion to a changed reality, but also a resolution of the struggle between the poets of blame and praise, Clytemnestra and Electra, who each tried to establish a version of the past as true.[3] Neither woman was able to overcome the other. The decisive contest between rival poets comes about not between the two women, but between the two male leaders, Orestes and Aegisthus. In the final scenes of the play the audience see Orestes move back and forth between the illusions of the drama and the reality he seeks to change, as he ultimately triumphs over another dramatic poet, Aegisthus.

[3] See Chapter 2.

In the first recognition scene of the play, we see the movement from illusion to reality as Orestes changes from a player in his own drama into the true Orestes. When he enters, we see him as actor, as he addresses the chorus:

τίς οὖν ἂν ὑμῶν τοῖς ἔσω φράσειεν ἂν
ἡμῶν ποθεινὴν κοινόπουν παρουσίαν;

Electra 1103-4

Who of you would tell those within
that our longed for company is here?

Orestes plays the role of the man new to Mycenae. At the beginning of the play Orestes was, in fact, unfamiliar with Mycenae and needed the Paidagogos as guide (1-14). Now he is acting out a role that was his natural state just a few moments before. He is using what was a natural appearance earlier as a deceptive appearance now. Later, he will use Electra's appearance as mourner in a similar way. Once Electra has recognized him, Orestes will direct her to continue to play the part of mourner in order to deceive Clytemnestra (1296-1300). Mourning was a natural state for Electra earlier in the play, but unnatural after she recognizes Orestes. Thus Orestes, as director, has his players use what was once natural appearance and emotion to create the illusions of the drama. He takes what was natural and turns it into a fiction more powerful than the reality of which it was a part.

Electra's question, when she hears that Orestes has come from Phocis, shows her awareness, and hope, that the report of the earlier messenger, the Paidagogos, might be different from the reality:

οἴμοι τάλαιν', οὐ δή ποθ' ἧς ἠκούσαμεν
φήμης φέροντες ἐμφανῆ τεκμήρια;

Electra 1108-9

Ah, wretched me, are you bringing visible proofs
of the <u>report</u> [phêmê] that we heard?

The word **phêmê** has a range of meanings which includes
its use as a prophetic, and authoritative, utterance. It is used in
this way by Odysseus, when he asks Zeus for a **phêmê** 'omen'
and then hears Zeus' prophetic response as one of the servants
prays for the destruction of the suitors (*Odyssey* 20.100-105).
Or **phêmê** can be used to mean the insubstantial speech of
rumor (e.g., Hesiod *Works and Days* 760-62). Electra has
unknowingly suggested the truth, that the utterance of the
Paidagogos has both the insubstantiality of fiction and the
authority of prophecy.

As part of his deception, Orestes, in his response to
Electra, seems to dismiss the Paidagogos' **phêmê** as simply a
rumor:

οὐκ οἶδα τὴν σὴν κληδόν᾽· ἀλλά μοι γέρων
ἐφεῖτ᾽ Ὀρέστου Στροφίος ἀγγεῖλαι πέρι.

Electra 1110-11

I don't know about your rumor; but the old man
Strophius ordered me to bring news about Orestes.

Orestes dismisses the report of the Paidagogos and says that
he has been sent by Strophius, the ally to whom Electra
entrusted the young Orestes. By naming Strophius as the one
who has sent him, Orestes is suggesting to Electra that his
report is more authoritative than the Paidagogos'. The
Paidagogos had said that he had been sent by Phanoteus, the
enemy of Strophius (670). The report from Phanoteus had more
credibility for Clytemnestra, while the report from Strophius
has greater credibility for Electra.[4] For Electra, the man to
whom she now speaks must be one of the **philoi** since he brings

---

[4] For the relationship of Phanoteus and Strophius, see pp. 89-90 above.

The Final Contest 115

a message from an ally. While creating an illusion, Orestes is telling Electra the truth: he is indeed one of her 'near and dear'.

As in the messenger speech of the Paidagogos, so also in Orestes' reference to Strophius, we see the artist presenting the truth in the form of an **ainos**. Just as the earliest model of the poet/king, Odysseus, used the **ainos** simultaneously to reveal and disguise his identity, so Orestes, while playing the part of a messenger, suggests to Electra that he is an authority figure greater than the Paidagogos, and that he is someone closer to her, a truly **philos** 'near and dear' man.

Orestes has used words, the reference to Strophius, to give his report more believability than the Paidagogos'. Now, in answer to Electra's question of what the news from Strophius is, he uses the dramatist's other means of persuasion, the visual. At this point he introduces the urn:

φέροντες αὐτοῦ σμικρὰ λείψαν᾽ ἐν βραχεῖ
τεύχει θανόντος, ὡς ὁρᾷς, κομίζομεν.

Electra 1113-14

Bearing the scanty remains of the dead man in a small
urn, as you see, we bring him home.

Moved by the sight of the urn and having taken hold of it, Electra laments her brother's death, ending with the hope that she will soon join him in Hades (1126-70). Moved by her words and grief, Orestes is torn between the demands of his role as actor and the urgency of his feelings for his sister. Caught between the two, he momentarily loses control of words:

φεῦ φεῦ, τί λέξω; ποῖ λόγων ἀμηχανῶν
ἔλθω; κρατεῖν γὰρ οὐκέτι γλώσσης σθένω.

Electra 1174-75

Alas, what should I say? Where in speech should I go, being now at a
loss for words? For I no longer have the power to control my tongue.

In this scene of recognition, as he emerges from his theatrical role as messenger to his real role as brother, Orestes struggles with the difficulty of what to say in the moment of transition. Electra, overcome with emotion at the sight of the urn and its confirmation of Orestes' death, was unable to confine her speech to the iambic line and broke into lyric anapaests (1160-62). Similarly, Orestes, when he hears Electra's anguished response to his false story, loses control, not of meter, but of words themselves.

We can compare the uncertainty of Orestes' words here with the assurance of Orestes' first lines to Electra in Aeschylus' *Choephoroe*. Having heard Electra and the chorus discuss the possibility that the offerings at Agamemnon's tomb are his, Orestes comes out of his place of concealment to reveal his identity to Electra. For Aeschylus' Orestes, there is no uncertainty, no search for the right words. He simply steps forth and calmly commands:

εὔχου τὰ λοιπά, τοῖς θεοῖς τελεσφόρους
εὐχὰς ἐπαγγέλλουσα, τυγχάνειν καλῶς.

Choephoroe 212-13

Pray for the rest to come out well, as you proclaim to the gods
that your present prayers have been accomplished.

For Aeschylus' Orestes the first words of the recognition scene are a calm command and statement of fact. But for Sophocles' Orestes, the crisis of recognition is a verbal crisis. As his role shifts from messenger to brother, the crucial act for the player/director is to find the appropriate and effective words for the new character. Orestes sees the issue of the moment to be one of speech and authority; he fears that he has lost both words (1174) and power (1175).

It is through the ensuing dialogue, a stichomythia of question and answer, that Orestes gradually reveals his identity to Electra (1176-1219). As Electra realizes that this stranger is her brother, each line itself breaks into question and answer, as Orestes identifies himself with words of both sound and sight:

Ηλ   ποῦ δ᾽ ἔστ᾽ ἐκείνου τοῦ ταλαιπώρου τάφος;
Op.   οὐκ ἔστι· τοῦ γὰρ ζῶντος οὐκ ἔστιν τάφος.
Ηλ.   πῶς εἶπας, ὦ παῖ; Ορ. ψεῦδος οὐδὲν ὧν λέγω.
Ηλ.   ἦ ζῇ γὰρ ἁνήρ; Ορ. εἴπερ ἔμψυχός γ᾽ ἐγώ.
Ηλ.   ἦ γὰρ σὺ κεῖνος; Ορ. τήνδε προσβλέψασά μου
      σφραγῖδα πατρὸς ἔκμαθ᾽ εἰ σαφῆ λέγω.

Electra 1218-23

El.   Where is the grave of that poor man?
Or.   There is none; for the living there is no grave.
El.   What are you saying, child? Or. There is no falsehood in what
      I say [**legô**].
El.   Is the man alive? Or. If indeed I [**egô**] have breath.
El.   Are you that man? Or. Look at this signet ring [**sphragis**]
      of my father and learn if I speak [**legô**] the truth.

As the exchange falls into a pattern of Electra's question in the first half of the line and Orestes' response in the second (1220-22), we have the sense of Orestes as the man who is able to finish the line, the artist who has the appropriate and final word. With the rhyme of **legô** 'I speak' and **egô** 'I' at the end of two succeeding lines and **legô** again at the end of Orestes' next response—**legô** (1220), **egô** (1221), and **legô** (1223)—Orestes, by means of verbal play, the tool of the poet, equates himself, **egô**, with the act of speech, **legô**.

It is not, however, simply the verbal play that reveals Orestes' nature to Electra. The object that Orestes uses to establish his identity is the **sphragis** 'signet ring' of his father, Agamemnon. To repeat, the **sphragis** is a much different recognition token from those used in other accounts of the story of Orestes' return. In the most famous of the versions that precede Sophocles', Aeschylus' *Choephoroe*, Orestes reveals his identity to Electra by locks of hair, footprints, and fabric woven by Electra herself (*Choephoroe* 164-234). The recognition tokens in Aeschylus are all signs of the connection between Orestes and Electra.

In addition to Aeschylus' play, there were other versions, known only in antiquity, of the recognition scene that preceded Sophocles', including those of Hesiod, Xanthus, Stesichorus, and Simonides. Of these we know something of the details of the recognition scene only in the work of Stesichorus. A papyrus fragment of a commentary on the poem (Stesichorus PMG 217) indicates that the lock of hair was used in this recognition scene also. In Euripides' *Electra*, which may have preceded Sophocles', the scar on Orestes' brow, the mark of a childhood accident, identifies him (573-74). As a child, while chasing a fawn in the courtyard with Electra, he fell, cutting his brow and receiving the scar by which he now proves his identity to his sister.

In all these versions the recognition tokens connect Orestes and Electra, through shared physical resemblance or shared childhood experience. But in Sophocles' *Electra* the token is different. The **sphragis** marks the connection, not between Orestes and his sister, but between Orestes and his father. The sight of the signet ring of Agamemnon authenticates Orestes' words, his claim that he is Orestes—τήνδε προσβλέψασά μου/σφραγῖδα πατρὸς ἔκμαθ' εἰ σαφῆ λέγω 'Look at this signet ring of my father and learn if I speak the truth' (1222-23). In establishing Orestes' connection with Agamemnon, the rightful ruler of Mycenae, the **sphragis** connects Orestes with the traditional and rightful source of authority in the community.

Looking closely at the nature of the **sphragis** as an object, we see further dimensions of its significance as the recognition token. In every day usage, the **sphragis** was used to make a wax impression that sealed an enclosure. As such, the **sphragis** was a much more important object in the past than can be imagined now:

Nowadays, when seal use is slight, when signets are rarely cut and even more rarely used, it is not easy to appreciate the importance attached to them in antiquity.... The basic purpose of sealing is to secure and identify property by so marking the sealing material that, if it is broken, it can be replaced only with the use of the same signet with its distinctive device. As a result of such usage either the signet or its device may acquire a special significance as the identification of the owner, and by gift of a signet authority may be delegated to a steward, messenger or subordinate officer.[5]

The unbroken seal assures the receiver that what is enclosed has not been tampered with. In the case of a letter, it proves the authenticity of what has been written. The particular symbol engraved on the signet ring that forms the impression on the wax gives proof not only of the authenticity of the enclosure, but also of the identity of the sender. The symbol engraved on the ring is associated with one person only. The **sphragis**, then, establishes two things: the authenticity of the enclosed written message and the identity of the sender.

With its two functions of verification of words and identification of their source, the **sphragis** authenticates that Orestes is the son of Agamemnon and assures his audience, Electra, that what he says is true. The **sphragis** at once establishes Orestes' connection with the authority of the kingship and establishes the authority of his words.

As we have seen, Orestes is like a dramatic poet, using the power of words to regain his position in Mycenae. The **sphragis** is another indication of Orestes' identity as poet, for the **sphragis** is a word of the literary tradition, the word that Theognis uses when he speaks of putting a 'seal' on his poetry:

Κύρνε, σοφιζομένῳ μὲν ἐμοὶ <u>σφρηγὶς</u> ἐπικείσθω
τοῖσδ᾽ ἔπεσιν—λήσει δ᾽ οὔποτε κλεπτόμενα,

---

[5] Boardman 1970.13.

οὐδέ τις ἀλλάξει κάκιον τοὐσθλοῦ παρεόντος,
ὧδε δὲ πᾶς τις ἐρεῖ· "Θεύγνιδός ἐστιν ἔπη
τοῦ Μεγαρέως· πάντας δὲ κατ᾽ ἀνθρώπους ὀνομαστός."

Theognis 19-23

Kyrnos, let a <u>seal</u> [**sphragis**] be placed on these words by me as I
practice my art and they will never be secretly stolen,
nor will any one exchange a worse thing for a <u>genuine</u> [**esthlos**] thing
that is here. And everyone will say: "These are the words of Theognis
of Megara. He is famous among all men."

The persona of the poet Theognis speaks of the **sphragis** (**sphrêgis** in the dialect of Theognis) as that which both authenticates words and identifies their author. The seal guarantees that the words are genuine, that no one has substituted something inferior for what is **esthlos** 'good, genuine' (21).[6] It identifies the poet Theognis as the source of the words of poetry (22-23).[7] When Sophocles shows Orestes using the **sphragis** to authenticate his words, he employs an object that connects Orestes with the power of poetic tradition.

With the realization that the man who shows her the **sphragis** is indeed her brother, Electra speaks of him in terms that are both verbal and visual. To repeat, when she sees the **sphragis**, her immediate response, her response of recognition, is to address him as the source of light and speech:

Ηλ.   ὦ φίλτατον φῶς. Ορ. φίλτατον, συμμαρτυρῶ.
Ηλ.   ὦ φθέγμ᾽, ἀφίκου; Ορ. μηκέτ᾽ ἄλλοθεν πύθῃ.

Electra 1224-25

El.   O dearest light. Or. Dearest, I join in the act of being witness.
El.   O voice, have you come? Or. No longer learn from any other source.

---

[6] For the meaning of **esthlos**, see above pp. 23-24, especially p. 24n29.
[7] For more on the seal of Theognis, see Woodbury 1952.20-41 and a reassessment in Ford 1985.82-95.

Electra equates Orestes with light and voice, the fundamental elements of drama itself. It is the **sphragis** that convinces her of Orestes' identity and causes her immediate association of him with things visual and verbal. In addition, as with all signets, the ring not only identifies, but also confers authority.[8] When Electra recognizes Orestes as the light and the voice, he insists that she learn this from no other source (1225), because the power and authority of Agamemnon have been conferred on him alone.

Through the character of Orestes, Sophocles shows the connection between authority and authorship. His Orestes establishes political authority through poetic authority. Orestes is like Odysseus, who uses the art of the epic poet to re-establish his kingship in Ithaca. Like the personas of the poets Hesiod and Theognis, Orestes works out **dikê** 'justice' in the course of his poetry—through the presentation of the drama itself. Like Solon, he combines the authority of the poet with the authority of the lawmaker. Sophocles shows Orestes as the dramatist who is the inheritor of the poetic tradition, having the verbal power of these poets, and more. For he uses not only the art of poetry to achieve **dikê**, but the power of the spectacle, the visual impact of the drama.

The *Electra* is a play about the nature of the dramatist and the work of art that he creates. It is an analysis of the role of the dramatic poet in the community and his methods—namely, his use of illusion and poetry—to establish his authority and to establish **dikê**. The significance of the **sphragis**, as an object, is that, like the *Electra*, it too is a work of art. It is a ring, a small piece of jewelry, beautifully crafted by an engraver. Made by an artisan, it puts an imprint, the image of itself, on the substance that seals an enclosure.

---

[8] See Boardman p. 119n5 above.

With the **sphragis**, Sophocles puts a seal on his own work. Many have told the story of Orestes' return, but with the **sphragis**, Sophocles identifies this version, this play, as uniquely his own. The **sphragis** is not simply the recognition token of the character Orestes. It is the recognition token of the play itself. The **sphragis**, itself a work of art, identifies the *Electra* as a work of art about a work of art, a play about playwrights and the art of writing the play.

There are many different views on the nature of the *Electra*, especially regarding its ending. Are there "Aeschylean echoes," as some suggest, or is it a "happy ending" play, with vengeance achieved in an Odyssean-like triumph?[9] With those who suggest that, given the authority of the Aeschylean version, Sophocles can never avoid those foreboding "Aeschylean echoes," this reading of the play differs. I suggest that, faced with the Aeschylean rendering that had eclipsed the Homeric version, Sophocles does not submit to this monumental vision, he defies it. His response to the challenge of Aeschylus' dominance is to attempt the seemingly impossible—to reassert the Homeric view of vengeance, justified and triumphant. As Sophocles' Orestes faces the challenge of Aegisthus as playwright, so does Sophocles himself enter into direct competition with his mighty predecessor Aeschylus. He reasserts the Homeric view of vengeance and then turns around to make his play something even more—a play about poetic

---

[9] For a sample of the range of viewpoints and bibliography, see Whitman 1951.149-71, esp. 162-63, where he maintains that the play presents a positive view of Homeric vengeance, but finds a different focus in the play than the one presented here; for the view finding significant "Aeschylean echoes" in the play, see Winnington-Ingram 1980.217-47; see also Stinton 1986.75-84, who differs with Winnington-Ingram, while still arguing against the "happy ending" interpretation; in addition, see Segal 1981.249-91 for his "darker view" of the play; for alternatives to these opposing views, see Roberts 1988.185-86 and Taplin 1983.163-64.

competition and the writing of a play. With the seal of Orestes Sophocles proclaims this story as truly his own.

After the moment of recognition with Electra, Orestes as playwright takes charge of the pace of the drama. He will not allow Electra to dwell on her version of the story in which she wishes to recount past sufferings (1281-87). He tells her,

> τὰ μὲν περισσεύοντα τῶν λόγων ἄφες,
> καὶ μήτε μήτηρ ὡς κακὴ <u>δίδασκέ</u> με
> μήθ᾽ ὡς πατρῴαν κτῆσιν Αἴγισθος δόμων
> ἀντλεῖ, τὰ δ᾽ ἐκχεῖ, τὰ δὲ διασπείρει μάτην·
> χρόνου γὰρ ἄν σοι καιρὸν ἐξείργοι <u>λόγος</u>.
> ἃ δ᾽ <u>ἁρμόσει</u> μοι τῷ παρόντι νῦν χρόνῳ
> σήμαιν᾽, ὅπου φανέντες ἢ κεκρυμμένοι
> γελῶντας ἐχθροὺς παύσομεν τῇ νῦν ὁδῷ.

Electra 1288-95

Give up excess of words,
and don't <u>teach</u> [**didaskô**] me that our mother is evil
nor that Aegisthus uses up the paternal property of our home
and squanders it and scatters it uselessly.
For your <u>speech</u> [**logos**] would get in the way of the critical moment of
timing. Indicate to me things that <u>fit</u> [**harmozô**] the present moment—
where, appearing or hiding, on our present course
we will stop our enemies, now laughing in triumph.

It is not for Electra to direct (**didaskô** 1289) Orestes.[10] Her **logos** would ruin their timing (1292). Having dismissed her speech, Orestes prompts Electra for the words that he wants, words that 'fit' (**harmozô**) the moment (1293). With the verb **harmozô** 'fit', Orestes uses a term which, as we have seen, is a word of both music and authority,[11] the appropriate word for the director to use as he asserts control over his actor and the

[10] For **didaskô** meaning 'teach' and 'direct', see p. 62 above.
[11] For discussion of **harmozô** in both its musical and political aspects, see pp. 26-27 above.

drama itself. Orestes intends, not to dwell on the past, but to move the drama forward (1294-95) to the next scene, the death of Clytemnestra.

These efforts are seconded by his mentor the Paidagogos, who comes out of the house and urges Orestes and Electra to cut short their speeches (1335). When Electra recognizes the Paidagogos as her old friend and Orestes' savior, she again delays the action in an out-pouring of joy (1354-63). Electra is portrayed here, as she has been throughout the play, as a woman who is expressive in words, but ineffective in action.[12] She is cut off in her speech of joy by the Paidagogos (ἀρκεῖν δοκεῖ μοι 'it seems enough to me' 1364), who tells her that there will be time later for stories of the past (1364-68). To the Paidagogos' call to act, Orestes responds by again taking charge of the play. It is time to move from the words of the drama to its actions:

> οὐκ ἂν μακρῶν ἔθ᾽ ἡμῖν οὐδὲν ἂν λόγων,
> Πυλάδη, τόδ᾽ εἴη τοὔργον, ἀλλ᾽ ὅσον τάχος
> χωρεῖν ἔσω,

Electra 1372-74

Our action should no longer be one of long speeches
Pylades, but rather, to go inside as quickly as possible ....

The men move on to the killing of Clytemnestra indoors and the confrontation with Aegisthus. In contrast to Aeschylus and Euripides, Sophocles places the death of Aegisthus after that of Clytemnestra. For Aeschylus and Euripides, the matricide and its implications are a central question, and the more important death, Clytemnestra's, is put last.[13] Sophocles uses a different order, since for him, it is not the death of

---

[12] See Chapters 1 and 2.
[13] See, for example, Whitman 1951.159-63 for discussion of the order of the deaths in the three plays.

Clytemnestra, but the defeat of Orestes' rival dramatist, Aegisthus, that is the greater concern. The audience see no direct confrontation between Orestes and Clytemnestra. Her death takes place off stage, and although the audience hear her cries (1404-16), they do not hear Orestes address any words to her. In contrast, there is an intense exchange between Orestes and Aegisthus before Aegisthus leaves the stage to meet his end (1466-1507).

When Aegisthus makes his entrance, the audience immediately see that he is a man concerned about words and stories. In his first lines, spoken to the chorus and Electra, he reports a report:

τίς οἶδεν ὑμῶν ποῦ ποθ' οἱ Φωκῆς ξένοι
οὕς φασ' Ὀρέστην ἡμὶν ἀγγεῖλαι βίον
λελοιπόθ' ἱππικοῖσιν ἐν ναυαγίοις;

Electra 1442-44

Which of you knows where the strangers from Phocis are
who, they say, announced for us that Orestes has lost his life
in a chariot wreck?

Some unspecified people say (φασί) that strangers have announced (ἀγγεῖλαι) that Orestes has died (1443). Aegisthus wants the report authenticated and turns to Electra. He is immediately the director, choosing his player, Electra, and, like Orestes (1293-95), prompting her to speak:

σέ τοι, σὲ <u>κρίνω</u>, ναὶ σέ, τὴν ἐν τῷ πάρος
χρόνῳ θρασεῖαν· ὡς μάλιστα σοὶ μέλειν
οἶμαι, μάλιστα δ' ἂν κατειδυῖαν φράσαι.

Electra 1445-47

You, I <u>choose and question</u> [**krinô**] you, yes, you, so
bold in former time; for I think it concerns you most
and you know best to tell me.

He directs Electra to speak, prompting her with 'you' (σέ) three times in one line, the third punctuated with ναί 'yes, you' (1445). With the verb **krinô**, which means both 'choose' and 'question', Aegisthus both chooses his player and forces her to speak (1445).

When Electra tells him that the strangers are within (1451), Aegisthus again shows that the words of the messengers are what interest him. He wishes to know what the strangers have said, what they have announced:

ἦ καὶ θανόντ' ἤγγειλαν ὡς ἐτητύμως;

Electra 1452

Did they truly report that he died?

In response, Electra improves upon Aegisthus' words. The strangers from Phocis have not simply said that Orestes is dead:

οὔκ, ἀλλὰ κἀπέδειξαν, οὐ λόγῳ μόνον.

Electra 1453

Not in word only, but they also showed [that he is dead].

Aegisthus expected only a verbal report of the death of Orestes; Electra stresses that the presentation is not simply one of speech, but also of sight. Orestes had used the prop of the funeral urn in the drama he presented to Electra. When Electra tells Aegisthus that the body of Orestes is at hand, Aegisthus immediately seizes on the same idea. He, too, decides to use Orestes' body as a prop in his own dramatic presentation, and so commands:

σιγᾶν[14] ἄνωγα κἀναδεικνύναι πύλας
πᾶσιν Μυκηναίοισιν 'Αργείοις θ' ὁρᾶν,
ὡς εἴ τις αὐτῶν ἐλπίσιν κεναῖς πάρος
ἐξῆρετ' ἀνδρὸς τοῦδε, νῦν ὁρῶν νεκρὸν
στόμια δέχηται τἀμά, μηδὲ πρὸς βίαν
ἐμοῦ κολαστοῦ προστυχὼν φύσῃ φρένας.

Electra 1458-63

I order you to be silent and to make a display by opening the gates
for all the people of Mycenae and Argos to behold,
so that, if one of them, by his empty expectations of this man
was raised up before, now, seeing the corpse, he
may accept my bit, and not, as a result of meeting my force
as chastiser, then develop good sense.

We may consider again the representation of the death of
Aegisthus on the Boston Oresteia Krater, in which Aegisthus
appears seated on the throne and holding a lyre.[15] At the
moment of his triumph, Orestes is shown overcoming Aegisthus,
who is holding back the lyre, as though to protect it. There we
see in the visual arts what Sophocles presents in the drama,
namely, that the man who controls music and poetry is the man
who controls the community. In Sophocles' *Electra*, the artist
Orestes controls not only language and music—the epic art of
the Paidagogos, the lyric lines of Electra—but he controls the
visual as well. The drama incorporates the artistry of epic and
lyric poetry and the power of the visual arts. The drama does
not simply, as Plato says (*Laws* 701a), absorb different literary
genres, such as here, epic and lyric; it also incorporates the art
of the painter. The dramatist uses the impact of the visual, as

---

[14] Here I maintain the manuscript reading σιγᾶν 'to be silent'—as do Jebb
1894, Pearson 1924, Kells 1973, Kamerbeek 1974, and Dawe 1984—in
preference to Wecklein's οἴγειν 'to open' and the change of word order that
Lloyd-Jones and Wilson 1990a and 1990b adopt.
[15] See pp. 1-2 above.

here Aegisthus expects to use the sight of the body of Orestes, to move the emotions of his audience.

Aegisthus is the director, ordering the eccyclema, with Orestes' body on it, to be rolled out. He expects to create a visual effect that will have the power to control his audience. He pictures the effect on the people of Mycenae when they see what he has presented to them, νῦν ὁρῶν νεκρόν 'now seeing the corpse' (1461). He expects to control them, like horses, with the bit that curbs the tongue (στόμια δέχηται τἀμά 1462).

In a similar context, Aeschylus has Aegisthus use the image of controlling the horse: τὸν δὲ μὴ πειθάνορα/ζεύξω βαρείαις, οὔ τι μὴ σειραφόρον/ κριθῶντα πῶλον 'I will yoke the disobedient man with a heavy yoke, no trace horse, barley-fed' (*Agamemnon* 1639-41). But Aeschylus' Aegisthus uses the image of the yoke on the neck, the image appropriate to Aeschylus' play. In contrast, for Sophocles' Aegisthus, the director who intends to control the speech of the players around him, the image of the bit that clamps down on the tongue is the appropriate one.

Responding to his order to show the body, Electra, like the Paidagogos in the messenger speech, now uses the ambiguous language of the **ainos**:

κὰι δὴ τελεῖται τἀπ᾽ ἐμοῦ· τῷ γὰρ χρόνῳ
νοῦν ἔσχον, ὥστε συμφέρειν τοῖς κρείσσοσιν.

Electra 1464-65

Indeed these things will be accomplished on my part; for in time
I have gained the sense to come to terms with the more powerful.

With the word τελεῖται 'will be accomplished', Electra employs the same verb that she used in reference to Orestes and Pylades when she reported to the chorus that they were about to kill Clytemnestra, τελοῦσι τοὔργον 'they will accomplish the deed' (1399). Here, to Aegisthus, she appears to be saying that she is following his instructions. But the audience know that the instructions she is really following are those of another director,

Orestes. As he ordered, she is hiding her joy and playing the part of the bereaved sister (1296-99). It is Orestes' deed—the overcoming of Aegisthus by the performance of the drama—that 'will be accomplished'. Similarly, when Electra speaks of 'coming to terms with' (συμφέρειν) the 'stronger' (τοῖς κρείσσοσιν) (1465), she uses a word of double meaning. The verb συμφέρειν, in addition to the sense of 'to come to terms with, to yield' can also mean 'to assist'. Aegisthus believes that Electra says that she is yielding to the more powerful, namely, himself and Clytemnestra, when, in fact, she is announcing that she is assisting the truly more powerful, Orestes and his **philoi**. Just as Orestes' first player, the Paidagogos, told an **ainos** to Clytemnestra, so now Electra, his other actor, plays her part by telling an **ainos** to Aegisthus.

Unaware that he is the audience of Orestes' play, Aegisthus continues to act as the director of his own. When Clytemnestra's body, covered with a veil, is brought out, Aegisthus directs that the veil be taken off:

χαλᾶτε πᾶν κάλυμμ' ἀπ' ὀφθαλμῶν, ὅπως
τὸ συγγενές τοι κἀπ' ἐμοῦ θρήνων τύχῃ.

Electra 1468-69

Loosen all the covering from the eyes in order that
kinship may find, even from me, the lamentation of threnodies.

With his order Aegisthus acts as the director in two ways. First, he is telling players what to do, namely, to remove the veil. And second, he is deciding how the visual elements of the drama will be presented. He wants the body to be uncovered in order to create the striking effect that he desires. In both respects he will be overcome by a director who is more effective than he. Orestes responds to Aegisthus' order to remove the veil, not by obeying, but by directing:

αὐτὸς σὺ βάσταζ'. οὐκ ἐμὸν τόδ', ἀλλὰ σόν,
τὸ ταῦθ' ὁρᾶν τε καὶ προσηγορεῖν φίλως.

Electra 1470-71

Lift it yourself. This is not my concern, but yours,
to see these things and to address them in a **philos** way.

It is Orestes who forces Aegisthus to remove the veil and make the corpse visible. Orestes the director determines the actions of Aegisthus the player, and the effect of the sight produced will be the one that Orestes, not Aegisthus, intends. Orestes' directions here to Aegisthus involve both the verbal and the visual. He tells him to act, to 'look' (ὁρᾶν), and to speak, to 'address' (προσηγορεῖν). When Orestes tells him to look, he is forcing him to be the audience of Orestes' play, not Aegisthus'. And when he tells him to speak, Orestes the playwright is creating Aegisthus' lines.

Aegisthus, now audience and actor in Orestes' play, responds to Orestes' order to lift the veil, acknowledging that he obeys:

ἀλλ' εὖ παραινεῖς, κἀπιπείσομαι·[16]

Electra 1472

You advise well, and I shall obey.

Yet Aegisthus still tries to take the part of the director. Though he could not make Orestes act, he still tries to direct other players:

σὺ δέ,
εἴ που κατ' οἶκον ἡ Κλυταιμήστρα, κάλει.

Electra 1472-73

[16] For παραίνεσις and αἶνος, see Maehler 1963.47 and Fraenkel 1950.339 vol. 2.

You there,
if Clytemnestra is somewhere in the house, call her.

Aegisthus is still ordering, and, like the director, ordering someone to speak, to 'call' Clytemnestra. He instructs his player to cause another character to come on stage. Like the playwright, he gives one player his lines and causes another to make an entrance.

In the confrontation between the two artists, Orestes, like his players the Paidagogos and Electra before him, now speaks in the form of an **ainos** to Aegisthus. When Aegisthus sends someone to call Clytemnestra, Orestes responds:

αὕτη πέλας σοῦ· μηκέτ' ἄλλοσε σκόπει.

Electra 1474

She is near you; no longer look to any other place.

The end of the line is similar in sound and significance to Orestes' response to Electra in the recognition scene, when she addressed him as the 'voice' and asked if he had come:

Ηλ. ὦ φθέγμ', ἀφίκου; Ορ. μηκέτ' ἄλλοθεν πύθῃ.

Electra 1225

El. O voice, have you come? Or. No longer learn from any other source.

Electra addressed Orestes as the poetic voice, and he answered that his was the only authoritative voice, 'No longer learn from any other source' (1225). He insisted on the verbal aspect of his authority. Now to Aegisthus, with a line remarkably similar in rhythm and wording, 'No longer look to any other place' (1474), he insists on the visual aspect of that authority. Aegisthus is to look at no other drama but the one Orestes presents. The dramatist invests both the words and the spectacle of the play with his authority alone.

Orestes has staged this recognition scene for Aegisthus, and he insists that Aegisthus be not simply a spectator, but a participant. He demands that Aegisthus remove the veil and look at the prop in Orestes' play, the body of Clytemnestra. Like Pentheus in Euripides' *Bacchae*, Aegisthus views the spectacle and, as a result of this experience, becomes a participant in it.

Aegisthus had expected to arouse fear in his audience and to force the realization that the long awaited Orestes was dead. Instead he finds that it is not his audience of Mycenaeans, but rather he himself who feels the fear and shock of recognition:

Αι.   οἴμοι, τί λεύσσω; Ορ. τίνα φοβῇ; τίν' ἀγνοεῖς;

Electra 1475

Aeg.   Alas, what do I see? Or. Whom do you fear? Whom do you not recognize?

Aegisthus sees, not the destruction of Orestes, which he intended to present as a spectacle, but instead his own destruction, and he wonders at its source:

τίνων ποτ' ἀνδρῶν ἐν μέσοις ἀρκυστάτοις
πέπτωχ' ὁ τλήμων;

Electra 1476-77

In the midst of what men's nets
have I fallen, wretched?

Orestes responds to Aegisthus' question with an **ainos**:

οὐ γὰρ αἰσθάνῃ πάλαι
ζῶν τοῖς θανοῦσιν οὕνεκ' ἀνταυδᾷς ἴσα;[17]

Electra 1477-78

---

[17] There are many different interpretations of these lines, with some editors preferring the emendation ζῶντας to the manuscript reading ζῶν (editors' preferences and interpretations are discussed in Lloyd-Jones and Wilson 1990b in their notes on line 1478). I follow Lloyd-Jones and Wilson in maintaining the manuscript reading ζῶν and have used the translation of line

> Don't you see by now
> that you, the living, are matching words with the dead?

This time Aegisthus understands the **ainos** and identifies Orestes as the speaker:

οἴμοι, ξυνῆκα τοὔπος· οὐ γὰρ ἔσθ' ὅπως
ὅδ' οὐκ 'Ορέστης ἔσθ' ὁ προσφωνῶν ἐμέ.

Electra 1479-80

> Alas, I understand this utterance; for there is no way
> that this is not Orestes, this man who is speaking to me.

The critical moment of recognition for Aegisthus is the moment of understanding the 'message', literally, 'word' (ἔπος), and identifying Orestes as the man 'who is speaking' (ὁ προσφωνῶν). In response to Aegisthus' recognition of him, Orestes refers to Aegisthus at this point as a prophet:

καὶ <u>μάντις</u> ὢν ἄριστος ἐσφάλλου πάλαι;

Electra 1481

> And, being the excellent <u>prophet</u> [**mantis**] you are, were you tripped up
> just now?

With regard to this line, it has been suggested that some part of the traditional story of Aegisthus has been lost:

> The line obviously implies that Aegisthus had some special qualifications in μαντική ['the skill of the **mantis**'] (cf. 1499). This is part of the backgound story which appears to have been lost.[18]

1478 offered by Kells 1973 on notes to 1477f. of the *Electra*, where he captures the competitive tone of the Greek.

[18] Kells 1973 at line 1481 of the *Electra*.

We know, however, that it is part of the role of the poet to be a prophet. The traditional poet is like Hesiod, to whom the Muses gave the ability to sing of both the past and the things to come (*Theogony* 32) and to whom they gave the scepter (30-31) as symbol of his authority to announce true things. "In effect, the figure of Hesiod presents himself as **mantis** ['prophet'] and **kêrux** ['herald'] as well as **aoidos** ['singer'] ...."[19] Originally, the poet was undifferentiated from the prophet and "the words **mantis** and **kêrux** ... could once have been appropriate designations for an undifferentiated poet/prophet."[20]

Orestes recognizes that poets are prophets and at this point is taunting Aegisthus with his failure to foresee Orestes' revenge. As Clytemnestra could not correctly interpret the **ainos** of the Paidagogos, so Aegisthus has failed to understand the drama of Orestes. A man who is not **sophos**, he has lacked the poetic skill to discern the true meaning of Orestes' play. Orestes has spoken in an allusive way, and Aegisthus has failed to recognize the evil that is to come. Orestes has taken the traditional role of the poet, whose words, as Theognis says, can be correctly interpreted only by the **sophoi**.[21]

When Orestes uses the verb σφάλλω to describe Aegisthus' failure to interpret the drama correctly, ἐσφάλλου πάλαι 'were you tripped up just now?' (1481), he is using an image from wrestling. The verb is used in a match, when one opponent brings down the other (e.g., *Iliad* 23.719). Like the account of the chariot race, where the Paidagogos told of a dramatic competition in terms of the athletic contest, so here, Orestes uses the image of the wrestler's fall to characterize Aegisthus' defeat in a contest of dramatic skill.

---

[19] Nagy 1989.23-24.
[20] Ibid.
[21] Theognis 681-82. For this passage in Theognis and Clytemnestra's inability to understand the **ainos** of the Paidagogos, see pp. 88-90 above.

The final contest for Orestes and Aegisthus has been a competition in presenting the most effective recognition scene. Just as the great poets Aeschylus, Sophocles, and Euripides must have competed with earlier versions of the crucial recognition scene in their own versions of Orestes' return, so Orestes and Aegisthus have each tried to outdo the other with rival presentations. Aegisthus had expected his audience, the citizens of Mycenae, to recognize the dead Orestes and, at the moment of recognition, to realize that they were now completely in Aegisthus' power (1461-62). Instead, Aegisthus, not the Mycenaeans, is the one to recognize Orestes, and the Orestes he recognizes is not the dead Orestes, but the living, triumphant hero. It is not the people of Mycenae who discover that they are overcome, but rather Aegisthus, who is defeated by Orestes in the very way that he had expected to overcome his younger rival.

When Aegisthus sees that he has lost, his first impulse is to beg to speak:

ὄλωλα δὴ δείλαιος. ἀλλά μοι πάρες
κἂν σμικρὸν εἰπεῖν.

Electra 1482-83

I am lost, a wretched man. But permit me
to say just a small thing.

Aegisthus, defeated by Orestes in his use of the spectacle of drama, now has one last hope: that he can still use the power of words, the verbal part of the dramatist's medium. Electra, however, interrupts, breaking into his line:

Αι.   ὄλωλα δὴ δείλαιος. ἀλλά μοι πάρες
κἂν σμικρὸν εἰπεῖν. Ηλ. μὴ πέρα λέγειν ἔα,
πρὸς θεῶν, ἀδελφέ, μηδὲ μηκύνειν λόγους.

Electra 1482-84

Aeg. I am lost, a wretched man. But permit me
      to say just a small thing. El. Don't let him speak further,
      by the gods, brother, and don't let him prolong speech.

Electra simultaneously demands Aegisthus' silence and, by her
interruption, brings it about. She not only forces him to be silent,
but then insists that after Orestes kills Aegisthus, he cast the
body 'out of our sight' (ἄποπτον ἡμῶν 1489). She realizes that
for Aegisthus to be overcome completely, he must be deprived
of the power of both the verbal and the visual, even in death.

In response to Electra's plea that Aegisthus not be allowed
to speak, Orestes, as he forces Aegisthus to exit, explicitly says
that he and Aegisthus have been engaged in a contest and
identifies the nature of the competition:

χωροῖς ἂν εἴσω σὺν τάχει· λόγων γὰρ οὐ
νῦν ἐστιν <u>ἀγών</u>, ἀλλὰ σῆς ψυχῆς πέρι.

Electra 1491-92

Go in quickly, for now it is not
a <u>contest</u> [agôn] of words, but a contest for your life.

Aegisthus had lost the visual battle in the contest of recognition
scenes. Orestes says that now the verbal contest is over, too.

Realizing that he has been defeated in the contest of
words, Aegisthus' one last effort as dramatist is to try to force
Orestes to kill him, not off stage, but on stage, before the
audience. Aegisthus, who could not control the spectacle of the
drama in life, hopes at least to have an audience for the
spectacle of his death:

τί δ' ἐς δόμους ἄγεις με; πῶς, τόδ' εἰ καλὸν
τοὔργον, σκότου δεῖ, κοὐ πρόχειρος εἶ κτανεῖν;

Electra 1493-94

Why do you lead me into the house? How is it that, if this is a noble
deed, there is need of darkness, and you are not now ready to kill?

Orestes again insists on control of the stage. He, not Aegisthus, will arrange the place of Aegisthus' death:

μὴ τάσσε· χώρει δ' ἔνθαπερ κατέκτανες
πατέρα τὸν ἀμόν, ὡς ἂν ἐν ταὐτῷ θάνῃς.

Electra 1495-96

Do not command, but go where you killed
my father, so that you may die in the same place.

Aegisthus still tries to prolong the discussion. For Orestes, the final point of the drama is the death of Aegisthus. But Aegisthus tries to expand the scope of the play:

ἦ πᾶσ' ἀνάγκη τήνδε τὴν στέγην ἰδεῖν
τά τ' ὄντα καὶ μέλλοντα Πελοπιδῶν κακά;

Electra 1497-98

Is it absolutely necessary for this house to see
the evils of the Pelopidae that are now and are to come?

Aegisthus is trying to turn Orestes' play into the Aeschylean version of the story.[22] He tries to force Orestes to view his death in the Aeschylean terms of the repeated sufferings of the generations of the house of Atreus, 'the evils…that are now and are to come'. To Aegisthus' question, whether it is necessary for the house to see the present and future evils of the race of Pelops, Orestes replies:

τὰ γοῦν σ'· ἐγώ σοι μάντις εἰμὶ τῶνδ' ἄκρος.

Electra 1499

Yours at least; of these I am the consummate prophet.

---

[22] For the question of the nature of the ending of the play, see pp. 122-23 above.

Like Sophocles, for whom Aegisthus' defeat in the poetic contest is the focus of the *Electra*, Orestes limits the scope of his play to the significance of the death of Aegisthus. Like Sophocles, he is not interested in the story beyond the moment of Aegisthus' death. He is intent on winning the dramatic competition and defeating the rival poet, as he emphasizes again the prophetic nature of the poet's power.

Aegisthus makes one more attempt to shift the focus of the play. Now he looks, not to future generations, but to the past, as he responds to Orestes' claim of being the 'consummate prophet' (1499) with his own taunt:

ἀλλ᾽ οὐ πατρῷαν τὴν τέχνην ἐκόμπασας.

Electra 1500

But you do not boast this as a skill inherited from your father.

But Orestes refuses to follow Aegisthus' lead in the dialogue. His play is not the Aeschylean version that broods on generations past and future. He insists that Aegisthus exit:

Ορ.   πόλλ᾽ ἀντιφωνεῖς, ἡ δ᾽ ὁδὸς βραδύνεται.
       ἀλλ᾽ ἕρφ᾽. Αι. ὑφηγοῦ. Ορ. σοὶ βαδιστέον πάρος.

Electra 1501-2

Or. You make many retorts, and our going is delayed.
But move. Aeg. You go first. Or. You must go ahead.

In the course of his confrontation with Aegisthus, Orestes has controlled first the visual aspect of the drama, defeating Aegisthus in the competition of recognition scenes. Now he controls the verbal aspect, limiting the scope and determining the end of the dialogue between the two players, Aegisthus and himself. In the closing lines of the play, he performs the final part of the director, orchestrating the last exit.

When he forces him into the house, Orestes demonstrates his complete power over Aegisthus. Orestes has in fact controlled his rival's movements since Aegisthus' first entrance. It was Orestes' play, the performance of the messenger speech by the Paidagogos, that first brought Aegisthus on stage:

τίς οἶδεν ὑμῶν ποῦ ποθ᾽ οἱ Φωκῆς ξένοι
οὕς φασ᾽ Ὀρέστην ἡμῖν ἀγγεῖλαι βίον
λελοιπόθ᾽ ἱππικοῖσιν ἐν ναυαγίοις;

Electra 1442-44

Which of you knows where the strangers from Phocis are
who, they say, announced for us that Orestes has lost his life
in a chariot wreck?

Just as he caused Aegisthus first to appear in the drama, now, in the final exchange, Orestes forces Aegisthus off stage:

Op. ἀλλ᾽ ἔρφ᾽. Αι. ὑφηγοῦ Op. σοὶ βαδιστέον πάρος.
Αι. ἦ μὴ φύγω σε; Op. μὴ μὲν οὖν καθ᾽ ἡδονὴν
θάνῃς· φυλάξαι δεῖ με τοῦτό σοι πικρόν.

Electra 1502-4

Or. But move. Aeg. You go first. Or. You must go ahead.
Aeg. So that I not escape you? Or. So that you may not die according
to your pleasure. I must keep it bitter for you.

Aegisthus, having failed in every other attempt at controlling the drama, here makes one last attempt, trying to control the final moment of the play. He tries to determine the order of the final exit. But in the rare double change of person in one line (1503), the audience hears his failure: he breaks into Orestes' line, ὑφηγοῦ 'You go first', but is immediately cut off, as Orestes claims the end of the line, and the final exit, as his own, σοὶ βαδιστέον πάρος 'You must go ahead'. Challenged one last time by Aegisthus, who tauntingly questions Orestes' motive for making him go first, 'So that I not escape you?' Orestes reiterates his position one last time, 'So that you may not die according to your pleasure.' Orestes will not allow Aegisthus any control over any aspect of his death.

Orestes has defeated Aegisthus in all the elements of the drama. He has determined entrances and exits. He has created a recognition scene so powerful that even his rival has been forced to look at his and no other play, μηκέτ' ἄλλοσε σκόπει (1474). He has controlled the speech of the characters in the play, even Aegisthus', as he cuts him off and forces him off stage. When Orestes takes away Aegisthus' control over the words and spectacle of the drama, when, by forcing his exit, he deprives the playwright of his audience, he has destroyed Aegisthus' power, reducing him to a player in Orestes' own production. At the moment that Orestes forces Aegisthus, his political and poetic rival, off the stage to meet his death, he has achieved, through the playwright's art, final and complete control over the kingdom of Mycenae.

Bibliography

Adams, S. M. 1957. *Sophocles the Playwright*. Toronto.

Alexiou, M. 1974. *The Ritual Lament in Greek Tradition*. Cambridge.

Arnott, P. 1959. *Introduction to the Greek Theater*. London.

_____. 1962. *Greek Scenic Conventions in the Fifth Century*. Oxford.

_____. 1971. *The Ancient Greek and Roman Theater*. New York.

Austin, J. L. 1962. *How to Do Things with Words*. Oxford.

Austin, N. 1975. *Archery at the Dark of the Moon: Poetic Problems in Homer's Odyssey*. Berkeley and Los Angeles.

Bain, D. 1977. *Actors and Audience*. Oxford.

Baldry, H. C. 1971. *The Greek Tragic Theater*. London.

Benveniste, E. 1969. *Le vocabulaire des institutions indo-européennes*. 2 vols. Paris. Translated by E. Palmer. 1973. London and Coral Gables, Florida.

141

Bernard-Moulin, R. 1966. *L'élément homérique chez les personnages de Sophocle.* Aix-en-Provence.

Bieber, M. 1954. "The Entrance and Exits of Actors and Chorus in Greek Plays." *American Journal of Archaeology* 58:277-84.

Blundell, M. W. 1989. *Helping Friends and Harming Enemies.* Cambridge.

Boardman, J. 1970. *Greek Gems and Finger Rings: Early Bronze Age to Late Classical.* London.

Bowra, C. M. 1944. *Sophoclean Tragedy.* Oxford.

_____. 1953. *Problems in Greek Poetry.* Oxford.

Brooke, I. 1962. *Costume in Greek Classic Drama.* London.

Burkert, W. 1977. *Griechische Religion der archaischen und klassischen Epoche.* Stuttgart. Translated as *Greek Religion,* by J. Raffan. 1985. Cambridge.

Burton, R. W. B. 1980. *The Chorus in Sophocles' Tragedies.* Oxford.

Buxton, R. G. A. 1982. *Persuasion in Greek Tragedy.* Cambridge.

Calame, C. 1977. *Les choeurs de jeunes filles en Grèce archaïque I: Morphologie, fonction religieuse et sociale.* Rome.

Calder, W. M. 1963. "The End of Sophocles' *Electra.*" *Greek, Roman, and Byzantine Studies* 4:213-6.

Campbell, L., ed. 1881. *The Plays and Fragments of Sophocles.* Oxford.

Clairmont, C. M. 1966. "Zum Oresteia-Krater in Boston." *Antike Kunst* 9:125-7.

Dain, A. and Mazon, P., eds. 1955-60. *Sophocle.* 3 vols. Paris.

Dale, A. M. 1969. *Collected Papers*. Cambridge.

Davidson, J. F. 1989. "Homer and Sophocles' *Electra*." *Bulletin of the Institute of Classical Studies* 35:45-72.

Davies, M. I. 1969. "Thoughts on the *Oresteia* before Aischylos." *Bulletin de Correspondance Hellénique* 93:214-60.

Dawe, R. D. 1973-8. *Studies in the Text of Sophocles*. 3 vols. Leiden.

_____. ed. 1975-85. *Sophoclis Tragoediae*. 2 vols. Leipzig.

Detienne, M. 1973. *Les maîtres de vérité dans la Grèce archaïque*. 2nd ed. Paris.

Devereux, G. 1976. *Dreams in Greek Tragedy*. Berkeley.

Diller, H. 1957. "Menschendarstellung und Handlungsführung bei Sophokles." *Antike und Abendland* 6:157-69.

Dodds, E. R. 1966. "On Misunderstanding the *Oedipus Rex*." *Greece and Rome* 13.37-49.

Dumézil, G. 1969. *Idées romaines*. Paris.

Dyer, R. R. 1967. "The Iconography of the *Oresteia* after Aeschylus." *American Journal of Archaeology* 71:175-6.

Easterling, P. 1977. "Character in Sophocles." *Greece and Rome* 24:121-9. Also appears in *Greek Tragedy*, 1993, edited by I. McAuslan and P. Wolcot in *Greece and Rome Studies*, vol. 2, 58-65. Oxford.

_____. 1978. "*Philoctetes* and Modern Criticism." *Illinois Classical Studies* 3:27-39.

_____. 1981. "The End of the *Trachiniae*." *Illinois Classical Studies* 6:56-74.

_____. 1984. "The Tragic Homer." *Bulletin of the Institute of Classical Studies* 31:1-8.

Edmunds, L. 1985. "The Genre of Theognidean Poetry." In *Theognis of Megara: Poetry and the Polis*, edited by T. J. Figueira and G. Nagy, 96-111. Baltimore.

Else, G. F. 1965. *The Origin and Form of Early Greek Tragedy.* Cambridge, Mass.

Erbse, H. 1978. "Zur Elektra des Sophokles." *Hermes* 106:284-300.

Faust, M. 1969. "Metaphorische Schimpfwörter." *Indogermanische Forschungen* 74:54-125.

_____. 1970. "Die künstlerische Verwendung von ΚΥΩΝ 'Hund' in den homerischen Epen." *Glotta* 48:8-31.

Fergusson, F. 1949. *The Idea of a Theater.* Princeton.

Figueira, T. J. and Nagy, G., eds. 1985. *Theognis of Megara: Poetry and the Polis.* Baltimore.

Flickinger, R. C. 1936. *The Greek Theater and its Drama.* 4th ed. Chicago.

Foley, H. P. 1985. *Ritual Irony: Poetry and Sacrifice in Euripides.* Ithaca.

Ford, A. L. 1985. "The Seal of Theognis: The Politics of Authorship in Archaic Greece." In *Theognis of Megara: Poetry and the Polis*, edited by T. J. Figueira and G. Nagy, 82-95. Baltimore.

Fraenkel, E., ed. 1950. *Aeschylus: Agamemnon.* 3 vols. Oxford.

Gellie, G. H. 1972. *Sophocles: A Reading.* Melbourne.

Gentili, B. 1985. *Poesia e pubblico nella grecia antica. Da Omero al V secolo.* Rome and Bari. Translated by A. T. Cole. 1988. Baltimore.

Goldhill, S. 1986. *Reading Greek Tragedy.* Cambridge.

_____. 1991. *The Poet's Voice: Essays on Poetics and Greek Literature.* Cambridge.

Goldman, H. 1910. "The *Oresteia* of Aeschylus as Illustrated by Greek Vase Painting." *Harvard Studies in Classical Philology* 2:111-59.

Gould, J. 1983. "Homeric Epic and the Tragic Moment." In *Aspects of Epic,* edited by T. Winnifrith, P. Murray, and K. W. Gransden, 32-45. London.

_____. 1985. "Tragedy in Performance." In *The Cambridge History of Classical Literature* I, edited by P. E. Easterling and B. M. W. Knox, 263-81. Cambridge.

Greengard, C. 1987. *Theater in Crisis: Sophocles' Reconstruction of Genre and Politics in Philoctetes.* Amsterdam.

Griffith, J. G. 1967. "Aegisthus Citharista." *American Journal of Archaeology* 71:176-7.

Hammond, N. G. L. 1972. "The Conditions of Dramatic Production to the Death of Aeschylus." *Greek, Roman, and Byzantine Studies* 13:307-450.

Haslam, M. W. 1975. "The Authenticity of Euripides' *Phoenissae* 1-2 and Sophocles' *Electra* 1." *Greek, Roman, and Byzantine Studies* 16:149-74.

Jebb, R. C., ed. 1883-1900. *Sophocles: The Plays and Fragments.* 7 vols. Cambridge.

Jens, W. 1971. *Die Bauformen der griechischen Tragödie.* Munich.

Johansen, H. F. 1964. "Die *Elektra* des Sophokles: Versuch einer neuen Deutung." *Classica et Mediaevalia* 25:8-32.

Kamerbeek, J. C., ed. 1953-84. *The Plays of Sophocles.* 7 vols. Leiden.

Kells, J. H., ed. 1973. *Sophocles' Electra*. Cambridge.

Kirkwood, G. M. 1942. "Two Structural Features of Sophocles' *Electra*." *Transactions and Proceedings of the American Philological Association* 73:86-95.

_____. 1958. *A Study of Sophoclean Drama*. Ithaca.

Kitto, H. D. F. 1956. *Form and Meaning in Drama*. London.

_____. 1958. *Sophocles: Dramatist and Philosopher*. London.

_____. 1961. *Greek Tragedy: A Literary Study*. 3rd ed. New York.

Kitzinger, R. 1991. "Why Mourning Becomes Electra." *Classical Antiquity* 10:298-327.

Knox, B. M. W. 1964. *The Heroic Temper: Studies in Sophoclean Tragedy*. Berkeley.

_____. 1979. *Word and Action: Essays on the Ancient Theater*. Baltimore.

Lattimore, R. 1951. *The Iliad of Homer*. Translation. Chicago.

_____. 1965. *The Odyssey of Homer*. Translation. New York.

Lesky, A. 1964. *Die griechische Tragödie*. 5th ed. Stuttgart. Translated by H.A. Frankfort. 1978. London.

_____. 1972. *Die Tragische Dichtung der Hellenen*. Göttingen. Translated by M. Dillon. 1983. New Haven and London.

Levine, D. B. 1987. "Flens Matrona et Meretrices Gaudentes: Penelope and Her Maids." *Classical World* 81:23-7.

Liddell, H. G., Scott, R., and Stuart Jones, H., eds. 1940. *Greek-English Lexicon*. 9th ed. Oxford.

Linforth, I. M. 1963. "Electra's Day in the Tragedy of Sophocles." *University of California Publications in Classical Philology* 19:89-126.

Lloyd-Jones, H. and Wilson, N. G., eds. 1990a. *Sophoclis Fabulae.* Oxford.

_____. 1990b. *Sophoclea: Studies on the Text of Sophocles.* Oxford.

Loraux, N. 1981. *L'Invention d'Athènes: Histoire de l'oraison funèbre dans la cité classique.* Paris and New York. Translated as *The Invention of Athens: The Funeral Oration in the Classical City,* by A. Sheridan. 1986. Cambridge, Mass. and London.

_____. 1985. *Façons tragiques de tuer une femme.* Paris. Translated as *Tragic Ways of Killing a Woman,* by A. Forster. 1987. Cambridge, Mass. and London.

_____. 1990. *Les mères en deuil.* Paris. Translated as *Mothers in Mourning,* by D. Glassman. 1992. London and New York.

Maehler, H. 1963. *Die Auffassung des Dichterberufs im frühen Griechentum bis zur Zeit Pindars. Hypomnemata* 3. Göttingen.

Martin, R. P. 1989. *The Language of Heroes: Speech and Performance in the Iliad.* Ithaca, New York, and London.

Mastronarde, D. J. 1979. *Contact and Discontinuity.* Berkeley and Los Angeles.

McAuslan, I. and Wolcot, P., eds. 1993. *Greek Tragedy. Greece and Rome Studies.* vol. 2. Oxford.

Minadeo, R. W. 1967. "Plot, Theme and Meaning in Sophocles' *Electra.*" *Classica et Mediaevalia* 28:114-42.

Nagy, G. 1974. *Comparative Studies in Greek and Indic Meter.* Cambridge, Mass.

_____. 1979. *The Best of the Achaeans.* Baltimore.

_____. 1982. "Theognis of Megara: The Poet as Seer, Pilot, and Revenant." *Arethusa* 15:109-27.

_____. 1985. "Theognis and Megara: A Poet's Vision of His City." In *Theognis of Megara: Poetry and the Polis*, edited by T. J. Figueira and G. Nagy, 22-81. Baltimore.

_____. 1989. "Early Greek Views of Poets and Poetry." In *Cambridge History of Literary Criticism* I, edited by G. Kennedy, 1-77. Cambridge.

_____. 1990a. *Greek Mythology and Poetics*. Ithaca and London.

_____. 1990b. *Pindar's Homer: The Lyric Possession of an Epic Past*. Baltimore.

Page, D., ed. 1962. *Poetae Melici Graeci*. Oxford.

Pearson, A. C., ed. 1924. *Sophoclis Fabulae*. Oxford.

Pemberton, E. G. 1966. "A Note on the Death of Aegisthus." *American Journal of Archaeology* 70:377-8.

Perotta, G. 1935. *Sofocle*. Messina.

Pickard-Cambridge, A. W. 1946. *The Theatre of Dionysus at Athens*. Oxford.

_____. 1968. *The Dramatic Festivals of Athens*. 2nd ed., revised by J. Gould and D. M. Lewis. Oxford.

PMG. *See* Page 1962.

Pohlenz, M. 1954. *Die griechische Tragödie*. Göttingen.

Prag, A. J. N. W. 1985. *The Oresteia*. Chicago.

Pucci, P. 1977. *Hesiod and the Language of Poetry*. Baltimore.

Radt, S., ed. 1977. *Tragicorum Graecorum Fragmenta*, vol. 4. Göttingen.

Reinhardt, K. 1947. *Sophokles*. 3rd ed. Frankfurt am Main. Translated by H. and D. Harvey. 1979. Oxford.

Robert, C. 1881. *Bild und Lied: Archäologische Beiträge zur Geschichte der griechischen Heldensage*. Berlin.

Roberts, D. H. 1987. "Parting Words: Final Lines in Sophocles and Euripides." *Classical Quarterly* 37:51-64.

———. 1988. "Sophoclean Endings: Another Story." *Arethusa* 21:177-96.

———. 1989. "Different Stories: Sophoclean Narrative(s) in the *Philoctetes*." *Transactions of the American Philological Association* 119:161-76.

Ronnet, G. 1969. *Sophocle, poète tragique*. Paris.

Rosenmeyer, T. G. 1955. "Gorgias, Aeschylus and ἀπάτη." *American Journal of Philology* 76:225-60.

Sandbach, F. H. 1977. "Sophocles, *Electra* 77-85." *Proceedings of the Cambridge Philological Society* 23:71-3.

Schein, S. 1982. "*Electra*: A Sophoclean Problem Play." *Antike und Abendland* 28:69-80.

Schneidewin, F. W. and Nauck, A., eds. 1909-14. *Sophokles*. Revised by E. Bruhn and L. Radermacher. Berlin.

Scodel, R. 1984. *Sophocles*. Boston.

Seaford, R. 1985. "The Destruction of Limits in Sophokles' *Electra*." *Classical Quarterly* 35:315-23.

Seale, D. 1982. *Vision and Stagecraft in Sophocles*. London.

Searle, J. R. 1979. *Expression and Meaning: Studies in the Theory of Speech-Acts.* Cambridge.

Segal, C. P. 1966. "The *Electra* of Sophocles." *Transactions of the American Philological Association* 97:473-545.

_____. 1980/81. "Visual Symbolism and Visual Effects in Sophocles." *Classical World* 74:125-42.

_____. 1981. *Tragedy and Civilization: An Interpretation of Sophocles.* Cambridge, Mass.

_____. 1982. *Dionysiac Poetics and Euripides' Bacchae.* Princeton.

_____. 1986. *Interpreting Greek Tragedy.* Ithaca and London.

Sheppard, J. T. 1918. "The Tragedy of *Electra*, According to Sophocles." *Classical Quarterly* 12:80-3.

_____. 1927a. "*Electra*: A Defense of Sophocles." *Classical Review* 41:2-9.

_____. 1927b. "*Electra* Again." *Classical Review* 41:163-5.

Shisler, F. L. 1945. "The Use of Stage Business to Portray Emotion in Greek Tragedy." *American Journal of Philology* 66:377-97.

Simon, E. 1972. *Das antike Theater.* Heidelberg.

_____. 1985. "Early Classical Vase-painting." In *Greek Art, Archaic into Classical*, edited by C. G. Boulter, 66-82. Leiden.

Snyder, J. 1976. "Aegisthos and the Barbitos." *American Journal of Archaeology* 80:189-90.

Solmsen, F. 1967. "Electra and Orestes: Three Recognitions in Greek Tragedy." *Mededelingen der koninklijke Nederlandse Akademie van Wetenschappen*, Afd. Letterkunde n.s. 30. no. 2:31-62.

Spitzbarth, A. 1946. *Untersuchungen zur Spieltechnik der griechischen Tragödie.* Zurich.

Stanford, W. B. 1983. *Greek Tragedy and the Emotions: An Introductory Study.* London.

Steidle, W. 1968. *Studien zum antiken Drama.* Munich.

Stevens, P. T. 1978. "Sophocles: *Electra*, Doom or Triumph?" *Greece and Rome* 25:11-20.

Stinton, T. C. W. 1986. "The Scope and Limits of Illusion in Greek Tragedy." In *Greek Tragedy and Its Legacy*, edited by M. Cropp, E. Fantham, and S. E. Scully, 67-102. Calgary.

Taplin, O. 1971. "Significant Actions in Sophocles' *Philoctetes.*" *Greek, Roman, and Byzantine Studies* 12:25-44.

_____. 1972. "Aeschylean Silences and Silences in Aeschylus." *Harvard Studies in Classical Philology* 76:57-97.

_____. 1977. *The Stagecraft of Aeschylus.* Oxford.

_____. 1978. *Greek Tragedy in Action.* Berkeley and Los Angeles.

_____. 1983. "Sophocles in his Theatre." In *Sophocle, Entretiens Hardt*, 155-74. Geneva.

_____. 1987. "The Mapping of Sophocles' *Philoctetes.*" *Bulletin of the Institute of Classical Studies* 34:69-72.

Torrance, R. 1965. "Sophocles: Some Bearings." *Harvard Studies in Classical Philology* 69:269-327.

Verdenius, W. J. 1962. "ΑΙΝΟΣ." *Mnemosyne* 15:389.

Vermuele, E. D. T. 1966. "The Boston Oresteia Krater." *American Journal of Archaeology* 70:1-22.

_____. 1987. "Baby Aigisthos and the Bronze Age." *Proceedings of the Cambridge Philological Society* 213:122-52.

Vodoklys, E. J. 1992. *Blame-Expression in the Epic Tradition*. New York and London.

Walcot, P. 1976. *Greek Drama in its Theatrical and Social Context*. Cardiff.

Waldcock, A. J. A. 1951. *Sophocles the Dramatist*. Cambridge.

Watkins, C. 1972. "An Indo-European Word for 'Dream'." In *Studies for Einar Haugen*, edited by E. S. Firchow, K. Grimstad, N. Hasselmo, W. A. O'Neil, 554-61. The Hague.

Webster, T. B. L. 1933. "Preparation and Motivation in Greek Tragedy." *Classical Review* 47:117-23.

_____. 1936. *An Introduction to Sophocles*. Oxford.

_____. 1956. *Greek Theatre Production*. London.

_____. 1959-60. "Staging and Scenery in the Ancient Greek Theatre." *Bulletin of the John Rylands Library* 42:493-509.

_____. 1962. "Monuments Illustrating Tragedy and Satyr Play." *Bulletin of the Institute of Classical Studies* Bulletin Supplement 14.

Weinstock, H. 1948. *Sophokles*. 3rd ed. Wuppertal.

West, M. L., ed. 1971/72. *Iambi et Elegi Graeci*. Oxford.

Whitman, C. H. 1951. *Sophocles: A Study of Heroic Humanism*. Cambridge, Mass.

Wilamowitz-Moellendorff, T. von. 1917. *Die dramatische Technik des Sophokles*. Berlin.

Wilamowitz-Moellendorff, U. von. 1883. "Die beiden Elektren." *Hermes* 18:214-63.

_____. 1914. *Aischylos: Interpretationen*. Berlin.

_____. 1921. *Einleitung in die griechische Tragödie*. 3rd ed. Berlin.

Winkler, J. J. and Zeitlin, F. I., eds. 1990. *Nothing to Do with Dionysos? Athenian Drama in Its Social Context*. Princeton.

Winnington-Ingram, R. P. 1980. *Sophocles: An Interpretation*. Cambridge.

_____. 1983. "The *Electra* of Sophocles: Prolegomena to an Interpretation." In *Oxford Readings in Greek Tragedy*, edited by E. Segal, 210-7. Oxford.

Woodard, T. M. 1964. "*Electra* by Sophocles: the Dialectical Design (1)." *Harvard Studies in Classical Philology* 68:163-205.

_____. 1965. "*Electra* by Sophocles: the Dialectical Design (2)." *Harvard Studies in Classical Philology* 70:195-233.

Woodbury, L. 1952. "The Seal of Theognis." In *Studies in Honour of Gilbert Norwood*, edited by M. E. White, 20-41. Toronto.

Index

72, 82-83, 86
Mycenae, 3-5, 13-18, 21, 23-25,
27, 29, 31, 37, 39, 46-48, 53-55,
58-59, 69, 87, 98, 102-104,
112-113, 118-119, 127-128,
135, 140
Mycenaeans, 63, 74, 132, 135
nightingale, 52
nikê 'victory', 48
oath, 30
Odysseus, 3, 6-10, 12, 20, 28-29,
37-39, 45, 57, 59, 70-71, 92,
114-115, 121
as beggar, 3, 6
and disguise, 3, 6, 28, 92, 115
offerings, 32, 34, 56, 68-69,
71-73, 81, 109, 116
ogkos 'bigness, bulk, padding',
21, 30, 93, 106-107
omen, 114
oracle, 28, 82-83
Orestes, 1-6, 8-48, 55, 58-65,
69-75, 83, 85-140
and Apollo, 28, 44, 83, 85-87
and kleos, 36
padding, 30, 93
Paidagogos, 3-5, 9, 11-31, 33-34,
36, 40-46, 48, 55, 62, 65, 72-74,
83, 85-109, 111-115, 124,
127-129, 131, 134, 139
paideia 'education', 11
parameters of the story, 91
Patroclus, 105
Pelopidae, 137
Pelops, 137
Penelope, 6, 70
Pentheus, 132
performance, 37-38, 46, 48, 61,
89, 98, 107, 110, 129, 139
Perses, 9

persuasion, 78-79, 115
phainô 'show', 22-24
Phanoteus, 89-90, 92, 108, 114
phaskein 'to say', 14-15
phatis/phatin 'speech', 62-63
phêmê 'utterance', 114
philos 'near and dear, friend',
22-23, 83, 88-91, 95, 99, 104,
109, 114-115, 129-130
philotês 'friendship', 53, 88
Phocis, 5, 87-89, 104, 112-113,
125-126, 139
Phoebus, 28, 82
phrazô 'say', 69
Pindar, 40, 98; *Olympian* 1.23:
40; *Pythian* 2.3-4: 98
plagai 'blows', 49
Plato, 33, 50, 91, 96, 127; *Laws*
701a: 127; 812d: 91; 816c: 91;
Phaedrus 278c: 91; *Philebus*
56a: 27; *Republic* 328a: 50;
377b: 33; 377d: 91; 379a: 33;
396b: 33; 396e: 33; 580b: 96;
Theaetetus 192a: 33; 194b: 33
play-writing, 6, 12
players, 9, 66, 113, 128-131, 138
playing, 1, 6, 59, 71, 107, 109,
115, 129
playwright(s), 3-4, 6, 11, 39, 41,
43, 60, 65, 74, 89, 91, 99,
122-123, 130-131, 140
Plutarch, 21; *On Brotherly
Love* 491a: 19; *On the
Generation of the Soul in the
Timaeus* 1029a: 19; *On
Progress in Virtue* 79b: 21;
Quaestiones Convivales 2.4:
94
poet, 3, 5-12, 14, 16, 19-24,
28-30, 32-33, 35-37, 39, 43,

About the Author

Ann G. Batchelder holds a Ph.D. in Classical Philology from Harvard University. She has taught Classics at Harvard University and is currently Assistant Professor of Classics at the College of the Holy Cross in Worcester, Massachusetts. Her fields of interest include Greek tragedy, epic, and ancient and modern rhetoric.